Class Assemblies for Primary Schools

Written by
HAZEL BENNETT

First Published
April 07 in Great Britain by

PUBLISHING

© **Hazel Bennett 2007**

The moral right of the author has been asserted in accordance with the
Copyright, Designs and Patents Act 1988

A CIP record for this work is available from the British Library

ISBN -10: 1-905637-14-4
ISBN -13: 978-1-905637-14-0

This Master may only be reproduced by the original purchaser for use with his/her students.
The publisher prohibits the loaning or onselling of this Master for the purposes of reproduction.

Typeset by Educational Printing Services Limited

Educational Printing Services Limited
Unit 6, Glenfield Park 2, Northrop Avenue, Blackburn BB1 5QH
Telephone: (01254) 686500   Fax: (01254) 686501
E-mail: enquiries@eprint.co.uk   Website: www.eprint.co.uk

Acknowledgements

I should like to thank the following for their suggestions and advice in compiling this book.

Samina Afzal
Jaspal Birdi
Indriyesha Das
Felicity Greenstein
Anna Hawkins
Pam Manku
(Imam) Mohammad Ahmad Ovaisi
Jaishman Shah
Judy Sitton
Dr Abdul Wahhab

Contents

Teachers' Notes

Why have *school* assemblies?	1
What is a *class* assembly?	1
Why have *class* assemblies?	1
Why have multi-faith assemblies?	1
How to go about producing a *class* assembly	2
The assembly scripts	4

Chapter 1 — Black & Asian history assemblies

Mary Seacole	1805-1881	5
Harriet Tubman	c1820-1913	11
Rosa Parks	1913-2005	16
Mahatma Gandhi	1869-1948	22

Chapter 2 — Buddhist assembly

Buddha Day	The first full moon in May	27

Chapter 3 — Chinese assemblies

Yuan Tan (Chinese New Year)	January/February	33
Dragon Boat Festival	May/June	40

Chapter 4 — Christian assemblies

St Valentine's Day	14th February	45
St David's Day	1st March	49
St Patrick's Day	17th March	54
Easter	March/April	60
St George's Day	23rd April	67
St Francis' Day	4th October	71
St Andrew's Day	30th November	76
St Nicholas' Day	6th December	80
Christmas	25th December	84

Chapter 5	**Hindu assemblies**		
	Ganesh Chaturthi	August/September	91
	Divali	October/November	95

Chapter 6	**Jewish assemblies**		
	Purim – The Story of Esther	March	102
	Pesach – The Story of Passover	April/May	106
	Shavu'ot – The Giving of the Ten Commandments	May/June	114
	Hanukkah	December	117

Chapter 7	**Muslim assemblies**		
	Birthday of the Prophet Muhammad		122
	Eid-Ul-Adha – Celebration of Sacrifice		126

Chapter 8	**Sikh assemblies**		
	Birthday of Guru Gobind Singh	5th January	133
	Birthday of Guru Nanak	April	137

Chapter 9	**Secular assemblies**		
	Rahere the Jester	d. 1144	145
	Blondel the Jester	Mid 12th century	149
	King Alfred the Great	849-899	153
	William Shakespeare	1564-1616	159
	Mother Teresa	1910-1997	164
	Bonfire Night	5th November 1605	172
	Bishop Gregory and St Augustine	540-604 (Gregory)	177
	Charles Dickens	1812-1870	185
	Boudicca	d. c60AD	191
	Edith Cavell	1865-1915	198

Teachers' Notes

Why have *school* assemblies?

A school is not merely made up of lots of individuals or even individual classes. It is essentially a community where each member is an important player and everyone works together for the benefit of others as well as themselves. School assemblies are an integral part of school life. They bring the teachers and pupils together to relax and enjoy the spirit of community life.

What is a *class* assembly?

A class assembly is one where a whole class performs for the rest of the school. Most schools invite parents of the performing class to watch. They often take the form of presenting a resumé of an interesting topic they have completed in class, an educational day trip or a presentation of a current religious festival. The aim of this book is to make the last one easy and enjoyable.

Why have *class* assemblies?

Although these are time-consuming to prepare they are well worth the bother.

- Pupils love to perform and have people to listen to them.
- It gives an opportunity to pupils who do not have much chance to shine in class and show what other talents they may have.
- Pupils who are attention-seeking in class often thrive in front of an audience so it gives them an opportunity to satisfy their need for attention in a positive way.
- Pupils can be nervous beforehand but overcoming their nerves to perform in front of an audience is an invaluable part of their education because it builds up their confidence and self-esteem. As all teachers know, success breeds success.
- Parents are often not aware of how much their children are gaining from the work of the school. Many parents are delighted to see their child perform with new confidence.
- Many teachers are nervous taking assembly. Some have told me they prefer class assemblies because the pupils do the performing and save them the task of standing up to address the school.
- In schools where there are regular class assemblies the practice often enhances the quality of end of year productions and Christmas concerts.

Why have multi-faith assemblies?

I have heard teachers of other faiths complain that during their childhood their teachers and classmates showed no interest in their culture because it was not standard British/Christian and at times this made them feel excluded. In many city schools, there is a wide mixture of religions, races and cultures. Creating a spirit of unity and community involves valuing all people and this, in turn, contributes to producing a happier, more tolerant and peaceful atmosphere.

How to go about producing a class assembly

Before you start

You will need to read the school policy on assembly. Every Local Education Authority produces an agreed syllabus for Religious Education and collective worship in state schools. Assemblies have to reflect the fact that the religious traditions of Great Britain are mainly Christian, while taking account of the teaching and practices of other major religions.
Voluntary-aided and foundation schools which are usually church schools write their own policies. Many schools have a majority of pupils of non-Christian faiths and so a policy of Christian based assemblies would not be suitable. These schools can apply to the local Standing Advisory Council on Religious Education for permission to have this requirement lifted.

Religious festivals

The Commission for Racial Equality (CRE) provides details of the dates and times of most religious festivals and celebrations. Many are movable feasts and so they have to be checked each year.

C.R.E.'s main office is at *St Dunstan's House, 201-211 Borough High Street, London SE1 1GZ*. Tel *020 7939 0000* or Fax *020 7939 0001*; Publications Dept *0870 240 3697*
or email *info@cre.gov.uk* Details of their local offices are on their website *CRE@tso.co.uk*

The Shap Working Party at *PO Box 38580, London SW1P 3XF*. Tel *020 7898 1494*,
Fax *020 7898 1493* or their website *www.shap.org* is another useful source of information.
In some religions the dates of festivals vary from year to year. A year by year calendar of religious festivals can be downloaded from *www.bbc.co.uk/religion/calendar*
www.google.com is, of course, a great source of information for any festival.

Guidelines

(a) Points to remember
1   The assembly should have an objective: a lesson to be learnt. The lesson does not have to be religious or moral, e.g. the objective may be to awaken the pupil's interest in the life and work of Charles Dickens.
2   If using someone's life and work as your theme, your objective might be to highlight the person's finest qualities – courage, service to others, willingness to defend the weak or use their talents for the benefit or entertainment of all.
3   The objective may be simply to give children an insight into another religion.
4   Whatever type of school you work in, you do not have to produce a religious assembly every time. A secular one is quite acceptable.

(b) The planning stage
1   Make it fun.
2   Always include everyone in the class. Children who have very little spoken English can have a miming part. Inclusion is as important here as in every other area of school life.
3   Try to give the less able pupils the best part they can handle. It works wonders for their self-confidence and self-esteem.
4   Try to split up the parts as evenly as you can. Keep a note of those who had the best parts in each assembly so that you share out the best ones evenly. It stops the parents complaining.
5   If you have pupils who play musical instruments, try to give them a chance to play in assembly sometime in the year, particularly if they do not have many other opportunities to play in public.

The prayer question

Unless the school has been awarded self-determination, there should be a prayer included. It is best to ask the children to write their prayer in groups and choose one or take bits from each one. If any pupils object to joining in a prayer, you can avoid an argument by telling them that it's no problem they can just sit quietly and listen without taking part. Some teachers tell the pupils to pray quietly in their own way and have a minute of silence, to avoid any friction about how children of different religions pray.

If parents object to their children attending assembly for this or any other reason, you might try saying, 'Of course you can withdraw your child but we hope you won't because it is an important community activity and your child is a valued member of our school.'

Whatever happens, it is never worth indulging in an argument with either parents or children because it generates more heat than light and then sets up ill-feeling. Remember that the keywords are 'fun' and 'community spirit'.

(c) Practising

1. Make sure everyone memorizes their part. Reading it never has the same effect. It won't matter if you have to prompt anyone who forgets their lines.
2. It is difficult to get the best performance from pupils until they have learnt their lines. Always offer generous amounts of house-points, stars, or whatever incentives your school uses, to pupils who learn their lines quickly.
3. Pay special attention to clear speech which can be heard at the back of the hall. Teach pupils to lower the pitch of their voice to raise the volume, and to speak slowly, pronouncing every syllable.
4. Have as many practices as you can fit in. It is not time wasted. The better the finished performance the greater the self-esteem and encouragement it will give the pupils for the future.
5. If you can tape a practice performance and play it back to the class it helps pupils to see or hear where they are going well and where they need to speak up or put more expression into it.
6. A performance with action is more interesting than a static one but some children find it hard to cope with simultaneously remembering lines, acting or speaking with expression and moving in co-operation with others. Starting with small amounts of movement and building up the action gradually with each practice often works well.
7. Primary school pupils often want to perform in costumes. This could lead to lots of extra work. If the school has no costume cupboard, tell the pupils that clothes don't matter but if they want one, they can provide it themselves.
8. Make it clear that speaking up clearly and acting well is what really matters.

(d) On the day

1. Have some music playing for the children as they are coming in and going out. Listening to something pleasant encourages pupils to sit quietly.
2. Have a drink of water ready in some discreet place, in case someone dries up during a speech. Of course you do not tell them it's available, otherwise they will all want it.

(e) When it is over

1. Mentally evaluate it. I always judge the quality by how much the class and the audience enjoyed it. Make a note of anything which you could do to improve it next time you use the script.
2. Keep an assembly file with all your notes, scripts, overhead projector (ohp) acetates, floppy discs (with PowerPoint data) and information taken from the Internet. It is all reusable after a few years.
3. Shower the class with lots of praise, house points or stars. Remember you need to keep their enthusiasm for the next one.
4. If someone is upset because they made mistakes, brush it aside and tell them that it was hardly noticeable.

The Assembly Scripts

The class assembly scripts in this book are written to save teachers' time by providing them with a bank of resources to fit a wide variety of occasions. Another aim is to share the parts out fairly evenly to everyone in the class.

The letter 'N' stands for narrator and each script has lots of them to make sure everyone can join in. Pupils can have more than one part.

You can have the whole class on the stage at once and pupils step forward to say their lines or perform their piece of mime or have them exit and enter as the stage directions suggest.

The great advantage of 'rhyme and mime' sketches is that you don't need any scenery or many props. As long as you keep the story moving onwards, people watching are happy to use their imaginations.

There are lots of songs and dance instructions on the market which make an entertaining assembly item, but it is not compatible with the copyright laws to reproduce them within this book. If you have pupils of a different culture, always ask them if they can perform a dance or sing a song appropriate to the theme of the assembly. I have often found they relish the opportunity and parents are often delighted to help them to prepare for it, lessening the burden on the teacher.

The assembly scripts end with a short, simple prayer, which you might like to use or, better still, ask your pupils to write their own.

Chapter 1 Black & Asian history assemblies

Mary Seacole

1805-1881

Mary Seacole's tremendous humanitarian contribution to the soldiers fighting in the Crimean War is an inspiring topic for a school assembly. For many years after her death, she was forgotten, but in the last thirty years her work has been properly acknowledged.
Children of all backgrounds can appreciate her amazing courage and generosity. Schools which take part in the Black History week may find this script useful.

Characters

Mary Seacole
Mrs Grant, her mother
Edward Grant, Mary's brother
Soldiers
A Medical Officer
Mr Day, Mary's cousin
Man at the War Office
Man at the Army Medical Corps
Assistant to Florence Nightingale
W. H. Russell
Army Surgeon
Lots of Narrators

(All of the class on stage. They can come forward at the appropriate time to play their part.)

N	Good morning and welcome to our assembly. We would like to tell you about the wonderful courage of Mary Seacole.
N	Who was Mary Seacole?
N	When did she live?
N	Where did she live?
N	What did she do?
N	Mary Seacole was born Mary Jane Grant in Kingston, Jamaica in 1805. Her mother was mulatto: she was a woman of mixed race. Her father was a Scottish soldier who was posted to the Caribbean. Mary and her mother had few civil rights. They could not vote, or hold a public office. They were even barred from going into a profession.
N	Mary's mother was not going to let that stop her. She was a nurse with a lot of medical knowledge for the period. She kept a boarding house in Kingston for soldiers who were wounded or were invalids. The soldiers called her the doctress.
N	Mary was a bright child who loved to learn and be involved in everything. We don't know if she went to school but we do know that she could read and write. Mary loved to watch her mother treating soldiers and she used her dolls to practise her

nursing skills.

(Mary's mother enters with a soldier who is supporting an injured arm. Mary, as a child, enters from the other side of the stage with a doll and a handkerchief.)

Mrs Grant   How did this happen, Lieutenant?

Soldier   I was on an exercise practising for war and I fell.

(She examines the arm and begins exercising it gently. Mrs Grant puts his arm in a sling and Mary copies putting the handkerchief sling on her doll.)

Mrs Grant   You're lucky it's not broken, but you won't be able to use it for a week. Leave it in the sling and rest it.

Soldier   It's dreadfully painful. I can't lift anything or even use my hand.

Mrs Grant   I can sell you some painkillers for it.

Soldier   Thank you Mrs Grant. Your medicines always work well. I don't know what the army would do without your doctoring skills.

Mrs Grant   *(Handing him a small bottle)*
You're welcome, Lieutenant. Now just be careful that you don't do anything with that arm. If it gives you any more pain, come back to me.

Soldier   God bless you, Mrs Grant.

Mrs Grant   You're welcome.

(Exit soldier)

Mrs Grant   What are you doing, Mary?

Mary   My baby has a sprain. I've put her arm in a sling. Can we go down to the beach now, Mummy?

Mrs Grant   Yes, let's go for a walk.

(They walk along holding hands, watching the events in the harbour.)

N   Mary loved to go down to the harbour and watch the boats coming in. She longed to leave Kingston and travel around the Caribbean and beyond it. When she grew up she did travel to Cuba, Haiti, the Bahamas and, of course, she wanted to see her father's country so she travelled to Britain. Mary loved it and in later life she wrote about her travels in a book called 'The Wonderful Adventures of Mrs Seacole in Many Lands'.

N   By the time Mary was twelve years old she was working in the boarding house, nursing the soldiers and learning about medicine from her mother.

N   When she grew up she managed to open a hospital for soldiers in Kingston.

N   In 1836, when Mary was thirty one, she married Edwin Seacole. Sadly he died in 1844, leaving Mary a young widow at the age of thirty-nine.

N   She travelled to Panama in 1851 to visit her brother, Edward. She was saddened by the illness and opened a hotel for the ill. There was an outbreak of cholera, and Mary managed to save people from dying of it. She got cholera herself and recovered from it.

N   During this time, Mary learnt a lot about medicine. She returned to Jamaica and found there was an outbreak of yellow fever.

(Enter Medical Officer)

Medical Officer
Mrs Seacole, thank goodness you are back. We have a dreadful outbreak of yellow fever. We can provide you with nurses. Can you please train them to care for and cure people who are suffering from this terrible disease.

Mary Yes, I'll start that right away.

N So Mary started her new task. By this time she had established herself as a skilled medical practitioner, in spite of being prevented from going to college because she was black.

N Mary had another idea. In 1853, when Mary was forty-eight, the British entered the Crimean War.

(Enter Edward Grant)

Mary You know, Edward, I'm really worried about all the soldiers who used to come here to my hospital. They're out there in Crimea in great danger. I am not there to look after them.

Edward You can't do everything, Mary. There is nothing you can do about it.

Mary Yes there is. I'm going to sail to England and visit the War Office. They are sending nurses out to Crimea and I am going to offer to go with them.

Edward But how will you persuade them?

Mary Surely with all my knowledge and experience, they cannot turn me down.

N Mary made the journey to England and went straight to the War Office.

(Enter man at the War Office)

Man at the War Office *(Looking at Mary with disapproval)*
We are very busy here. What do want?

Mary My name is Mary Seacole. I am a doctress from Jamaica. I have run hospitals and cured people of cholera and yellow fever. I would like to join your nursing team and go to Crimea.

Man at the War Office
But we cannot just take anyone to Crimea. Anyway how do we know you are telling the truth?

Mary *(Offering her references)*
I have references from the Head of the Medical Service in Jamaica.

Man at the War Office
Oh very well. Let me see them. *(He reads)* I still don't think we can send you out there with all our British nurses. Don't come here again.

(Mary leaves)

N Mary was not put off. Next she went to the Army Medical Department.

(Enter man from the Army Medical Department)

Man at the Army Medical Department
I'm busy. What do you want?

Mary My name is Mary Seacole. I am a doctress from Jamaica. I have run hospitals and cured people of cholera and yellow fever. I would like to join your nursing team and go to Crimea.

Man at the Army Medical Department
It's not possible. We need women of experience and with medical knowledge.

Mary I have been a nurse for many years. I cured people with cholera. The Medical Department in Kingston asked me to open a hospital to care for people with yellow fever and we cured people.

Man at the Army Medical Department
How do I know you are telling the truth?

Mary Read my references.

Man at the Army Medical Department *(flicking through them quickly)*
I don't think so. I have to go now.

(He hands back the references and rushes off)

N But still Mary was not put off. Next she applied to Florence Nightingale's assistants.

(Enter one of Florence Nightingale's assistants.)

Mary Excuse me.

Assistant *(Annoyed at having to listen to Mary)*
What do you want?

Mary My name is Mary Seacole. I am a doctress from Jamaica. I have run hospitals and cured people of cholera and yellow fever. I would like to join your nursing team and go to Crimea.

Assistant But we only take the best to Crimea.

Mary But you are short of nurses in Britain. I have many years of experience as a nurse and a doctress. Read my references from the Head of our Medical Services in Jamaica.

Assistant Oh all right. *(Reads briefly)* Don't contact us. We'll contact you if we want you.

N Mary goes off, hurt but not put off. She meets her cousin, Day.

(She greets Day in a warm manner)

Mary I can't believe this. It seems that the British have the same old prejudice against black people that the Americans have. I have cared for so many British soldiers in the Caribbean. I have cured people of cholera and yellow fever and these people think that I am unworthy because I have a darker skin than theirs.

Day I know, Mary. It's awful, but I think you will have to go home to Jamaica now. There is nothing here for you.

Mary No, I will not go home. You are going to Balaclava on business, aren't you? Won't you take me with you?

Day Yes, of course. But what can you do when you get there?

Mary We can start up a business together. I have a large store of medicines. We

	can find a property and start up a hotel for the wounded soldiers. We'll show them that they can't put us down.
Day	Right, let's do it.
N	So Mary went off to Balaclava with Day and they became sutlers. They are people who follow the army at war and sell them things which they need like medicines, food and boots. They bought a large house and set up their hotel near the town of Sevastopol and treated the wounded soldiers. They even risked their lives going to battlefields to rescue the soldiers.
N	Some people were prejudiced against her because she was black and because she had no formal qualifications. Others were kinder and appreciated her.

(In the background the class mime a battle-scene, in pairs, miming fighting. Mary and her assistants help the wounded off the field, during the next two speeches.)

W.H. Russell
Mary Seacole is a kindly and competent doctor, who treats and cures with wonderful success. She is never far from the battlefield to help the wounded and is blessed by many fallen injured soldiers.
This is W.H. Russell, war correspondent for the Times, in Sevastopol, Crimea.

Army Surgeon
I am an army surgeon. I have watched Mrs Seacole with ever-growing admiration. No matter how cold it is, she is always at the battlefield, ready to help any soldier with food, tea, words of comfort and ready to take them back to her hotel. She is often under the line of fire and completely fearless.

(Exit soldiers)

N	In 1856 the Crimean War ended. Mary and her cousin Mr Day, found themselves bankrupt. They managed to return to England, but they had no money. Fortunately they had friends in high places.
N	Two army commanders who had fought at Crimea organized a benefit concert for her at the Royal Surrey Gardens in Kennington in South London. It was a grand festival which lasted four nights, with over a thousand performers helping to raise a large amount of money for Mary to show their appreciation of her devotion to the British soldiers.
N	The Prince of Wales applauded her and Queen Victoria's nephew, Prince Victor who was a sculptor, made a model of her head and shoulders.
N	Mary was awarded the Crimean Medal, The French Legion of Honour and Turkish medal for her magnificent work in Crimea.
N	The following year Mary published her book, 'The Wonderful Adventures of Mrs Seacole in Many Lands'. W.H. Russell wrote the preface.

W.H. Russell
'I trust that England will not forget one who nursed her sick, who sought out her wounded to help them, and who comforted her bravest soldiers in the last hours of their lives.'

N	Mary Seacole died on 14th May 1881 and she is buried in St Mary's Catholic Cemetery in Kensal Green in North West London. Sadly England did forget about Mary Seacole. For many years only Florence Nightingale was hailed as the Lady of the Lamp for her excellent work nursing the soldiers at Crimea, while Mary Seacole was forgotten because she was black. About thirty years ago the memory of Mary Seacole was revived.

N   In 1994, the Department of Health provided awards for black minority ethnic nurses. An organization called 'The Friends of Mary Seacole' have made a memorial garden for her in Scrubs Lane near where she is buried. Now she will never be forgotten.

N   Let us pray.
Oh God our father, thank you for Mary Seacole. Help us always to be ready to help anyone in difficulty and to be kind to anyone who is in pain or in need of sympathy.

Chapter 1 Black & Asian history assemblies

Harriet Tubman

c1820 – 1913

Harriet Tubman, an American slave of African descent, was born around 1820. She showed outstanding levels of courage and determination in standing up to injustice against herself, her family and other black slaves. Known as the Moses of the black people for leading so many black slaves safely to freedom and for her work during and after the Civil War, Harriet Tubman is a worthy character to be included in an assembly in a Black History Month.

> **Characters**
>
> Harriet (Araminta, at birth)
> Benjamin Ross, her father
> Harriet Ross (Green), her mother
> Harriet's three sisters (non-speaking parts)
> Edward Brodess, owner of the plantation where the Ross family worked.
> Eliza Brodess, his wife
> Lawyer
> Slave overseer
> Another slave owner
> White friend
> Anti-slavery member
> William Still
> Slaves on the journey
> Bounty hunters
> John Brown
> All of the above, except Harriet can double up as narrators.

(The whole class on the stage to start. They can come forward, in turn, to play their parts.)

N	Good morning and welcome to our assembly.
N	We would like to tell you about Harriet Tubman.
N	Who was she?
N	When did she live?
N	What did she do?
N	Why should we remember her today?
N	Harriet Tubman was born in Bucktown in Dorchester in Maryland about 1820. In those days, some states of North America allowed slavery. This meant that white people could buy and sell black people and force them to work for them without any payment except food. Often slave-owners treated their slaves with great cruelty. Harriet's father Benjamin Ross and her mother Harriet Green had nine children. Harriet was their fifth. The family were slaves on a plantation owned by Edward Brodess.

(Harriet, the mother, sitting with a doll wrapped up in a cloth. Enter Benjamin.)

Benjamin Harriet, my dear, another girl. Well done. What will we call her?

Harriet Ross I'd like to call her Araminta.

Benjamin Araminta Ross. A sweet name for a sweet little baby girl.

Harriet Ross Our poor little Araminta is just another slave for the Brodess family to use and abuse. Will there ever be an end to slavery? Will we ever be able to live freely and live in peace with the white men?

Benjamin One day, my dear. One day our people will be free. One day someone will come and lead us to freedom. *(They exit.)*

N As Benjamin Ross smiled on his beautiful new baby daughter, he could not have guessed that she would be the saviour who would lead him and his family and others to freedom.

N When Araminta was six, she had her first taste of life as a slave.

Eliza Brodess Wash all those dishes and dry them and mind you don't break anything. And when you have finished, get a bucket of hot water and a brush and get on to your knees and scrub that floor and make sure you do it properly.

N Edward Brodess regularly made money out of Araminta by hiring her out to other plantation owners, who treated her and the other slaves cruelly. One day a slave tried to escape.

(Slave rushes across the stage pursued by an overseer. Araminta comes between them and prevents the overseer from catching the slave who escapes. Overseer picks up a 'stone' (sponge wrapped in brown sugar paper or equivalent) and throws it at Araminta's head. She falls unconscious.)

Overseer She dared to stop me. That'll teach her. Throw her into the slave house. If she dies, throw her into the pit.

N Araminta did not die, but she was unconscious for some time and for the rest of her life, she suffered epileptic fits, where she fell into a deep sleep for several hours.

N There was more cruelty in store for the Ross family.

(Enter Brodess and another slave-owner, three Ross daughters, Araminta and their parents.)

Brodess What will you give me for these able-bodied slaves?
(Points to Araminta's three sisters)

Benjamin Those are my daughters!

Brodess They will work all day. They are in good health.

Slave-owner Three dollars each.

Brodess Make it five each.

Benjamin But these are my children!

Slave owner Four dollars each.

Brodess It's a deal. *(Slave-owner hands over money, they shake hands. The girls cry as they hug and kiss their parents and Araminta to say good-bye.)*

Araminta You know, mother, I want to change my name. From now on I want to be called Harriet in honour of you.

N In 1944, when she was twenty-four years old, Harriet married John Tubman, so Araminta Ross became Harriet Tubman.

(Enter John Tubman. He stands beside Harriet, arm-in-arm.)

Harriet You are a brave man to marry a slave while you are a free man.

Tubman I am so sorry that marrying you cannot make you a free woman. It is such a harsh law that means our children will be slaves to the Brodess family. *(They exit)*

N In 1944 more trouble was in store for the Tubmans.

(Enter Eliza Brodess and her lawyer.)

Eliza Brodess I have terrible news. My husband, Edward Brodess has died.

Lawyer I'm sorry to hear that. You know, Mrs Brodess, your husband did not manage his money well. He had a lot of debts, which will now have to be paid.

Eliza But how will I do that? He has left no money.

Lawyer You will have to sell as much as you can.

Eliza But I don't want to lose our home. What should I do?

Lawyer You have lots of slaves, you will just have to sell them off. There are plenty of plantation owners in the Deep South who could use your slaves. You would get a good price for them and have just enough to keep the farm.

(They exit. Enter Harriet and her white friend.)

N This was terrible news for Harriet and her family. Fortunately she had a white friend who was opposed to slavery.

Harriet Have you heard what is going to happen? We might be sold and sent to the Deep South. I wish I could escape.

White Friend I can help you. Here is the address of a safe house for you. If you can escape and get there, they will help you to escape to a state where there is no slavery.

(Both leave the stage.)

N Harriet escaped and found the first address.

(Enter Harriet warily. She knocks on a door.)

Harriet My name is Harriet Tubman. I have escaped from the Brodess plantation.

Anti-slavery member Thank goodness you made it safely. We'll have to move fast. This will be an uncomfortable ride for you. You'll have to get into the back of the wagon and we'll have to cover you with bags in case we are stopped. If we are lucky we will get you to Philadelphia where you will be safe.

Harriet	Thank you.
N	So the brave man drove her to Philadelphia and freedom.

(Harriet and the man shake hands to part.)

Harriet	Thank you, sir, for taking the risk of bringing me to freedom.
Anti-slavery member	Good luck, mam. *(He exits)*
Harriet	I'm free at last. It's a wonderful feeling to be my own person and not just someone else's possession. I'm no longer someone's slave but there is no one to welcome me. I am a stranger in a strange land.
N	In Philadelphia, Harriet met William Still, the stationmaster on the Underground Railroad.
Still	Harriet, I am glad to meet you. I wonder if you would like to join us. I am a member of the Anti-Slavery Society. We have a list of safe houses between here and Maryland and we help slaves to escape. We call our organization the UGRR - Underground Railroad. We work with the Philadelphia Anti-Slavery Society.
Harriet	I certainly would. I would like to go back to Maryland and rescue my family.
Still	We can help you do that.
Harriet	Can you show me the nearest church. *(They both exit)*
N	Harriet was a Christian and she joined the local church. She believed that God was looking after her and would help her to bring people to safety. It was horribly dangerous because if they were caught, they would be returned to their slave owner and would suffer a horrendous beating.

(Enter Harriet leading an anxious-looking group of slaves.)

1st slave	How much further is it? I'm starving. We haven't eaten all day.
2nd slave	At least on the plantation we had food and water.
3rd slave	Walking all day, every day, is worse than working all day. Why can't we go back to the plantation?
Harriet	I'm not going back to the plantation! Where is your spirit? Don't you want to be free of slavery?
3rd slave	You go on with the others, Harriet. I'll go back alone.
Harriet	If one of you goes back you are bound to get caught. The police will beat you until you tell them where the rest of us are. If you leave you would put every one of us in danger.
3rd slave	No I won't Harriet, I promise you, I won't tell anyone about you and the others.
Harriet	*(Pulling out a toy gun)* You will live in freedom or die a slave.
2nd slave	You're meant to be our friend, Harriet. Why are you threatening to kill one of your own people?
Harriet	A runaway slave could put us all in danger, but a dead man gives no secrets away. *(They exit)*
N	During the ten years that Harriet worked with the Underground Railroad, she made

	nineteen journeys back to Maryland and rescued over three hundred slaves, including her own family.
N	She was known as the Moses of the black people because she led them out of slavery to freedom. In all that time she never lost one of her people on the journey.
N	She joined the Abolitionist Movement. That was an organization which was determined to stop slavery in every state in America.
N	The slave-owners were eager to catch her. There were large posters everywhere with her picture offering an enormous reward.

(Enter two bounty-hunters at one side of the stage and Harriet at the other.)

1st bounty hunter
Look at this poster. A reward of $40,000 for an illiterate black slave called Harriet Tubman.

2nd bounty hunter
That's the biggest reward I've ever seen for a slave. How can any slave be worth that much?

1st bounty hunter
Read what it says. 'This woman has been rescuing slaves all over Maryland and taking them to a state that doesn't allow slavery.' Plantation owners must be losing money all the time because of her.

2nd bounty hunter
We ought to make sure we find her. With money like that we could live nice and easy for the rest of our lives.

1st bounty hunter
Look at that woman over there. She looks mighty like this woman in the picture.

(Harriet takes a book out of her bag and starts to 'read' it.)

2nd bounty hunter
Too bad. Let's go off and find this woman. *(They exit)*

N	During these years Harriet Tubman's courage never failed her.
N	During the American Civil War, Harriet was still busy. She worked as a nurse and even a spy. After the Civil War, slavery was abolished, and she settled in the Auburn district of New York. Harriet lived until 1913, when she was 93 years old.

(Enter John Brown)

John Brown My name is John Brown. Before the American Civil War, I spent years fighting to abolish slavery. I met Harriet Tubman and she is one of the bravest persons on this continent.

N	Let us pray. Oh God, thank you for Harriet Tubman's example of courage in standing up to evil. Please bring an end to the evil system of slavery which still exists in some parts of the world. Help us always to be brave enough to stand up for people who are in difficulty and always to speak up against things which we know are wrong.

Chapter 1 Black & Asian history assemblies

Rosa Parks

1913 – 2005

Rosa Parks' death on 24th October 2005 reminded everyone of her contribution to the American Civil Rights Movement. She will always be remembered as the woman who showed courage and dignity in standing up to injustice and triggering off the movement which brought freedom and justice to black Americans.
This script takes the form of an interview between Rosa as a senior citizen, while a young Rosa acts out her story. Old Rosa can read the parts from her manuscript to make it easier.

Characters

Rosa Parks as an old woman
Rosa Parks as a child and a young woman
Leona McCauley, her mother
Grandad and Grandmother
Journalist
Policeman
Raymond Parks, Rosa's husband
James Blake, the bus driver
Rev. Abernathy
Dr Martin Luther King
People in the Ku Klux Klan
People on the bus
People in the courtroom
People at the black protest meeting
Narrators

N   Good morning and welcome to our assembly. Today we would like to tell you about Rosa Parks, a black woman who grew up in Montgomery in Alabama in the 1920s.

(Rosa, as an old lady almost eighty in 1992, is sitting on a chair at the side of the stage reading a manuscript of white A4 paper. The journalist enters.)

Journalist   You look pleased, Rosa. What are you reading?

Old Rosa   I've written some of the first draft of my autobiography. It's called Rosa Parks: My Story.

Journalist   That's a great idea. Rosa. Read it to me.

(Rosa begins reading while a young Rosa enters the stage from the other side holding her mother's hand.)

Old Rosa   I was born Rosa Louise McCauley in Tuskgee on 4th February 1913 in Alabama. My father James McCauley was a carpenter and my mother Leona McCauley was a teacher. Unfortunately they did not stay together and when we were still small, my mother took my brother Sylvester and I to live with her parents on their farm at Pine Level just outside Montgomery, Alabama. The fresh country air was good for my health because I was often ill. As I grew up I learned all about the laws against black people.

Rosa *(as a child)*
Mom, why can't we go to that playground to play.

Leona   Because it's just for white children.

Rosa   But Mom, I'd like to play there too.

Leona   I'm sorry, darling. Black people and white people have to stay separate in Alabama.

Rosa   That's not fair.

Leona   I know it's not fair, but there doesn't seem to be much we can do about it.

Old Rosa   The Ku Klux Klan occasionally walked down the road past our house.

(Most of the rest of class walk across the stage in front of Young Rosa's family. They all have their faces covered by a white cloth with holes cut for eyes.)

Young Rosa   Grandma, who are those people?

Grandma   They're the Ku Klux Klan.

Young Rosa   Why are they dressed like that? Why have they got their heads covered up?

Grandma   Because they are cowards. They don't want anyone to see their faces.

Young Rosa   What do they want?

Grandma   They want to get rid of us black people. They think we have no right to live here.

Young Rosa   Grandad, why have you got your shotgun out?

Grandad   If one of those guys comes anywhere near our house I'm going to shoot him.
(They move off stage.)

Journalist   Did you go to school, Rosa?

Old Rosa   My mother taught me at home until I was eleven. Remember, she was a teacher. *(Reading from her manuscript)* In those days, there were laws known as the Jim Crow laws. Black people were separated from white people in everything.
There were no buses to take black children to school in the south where we lived. They had a law that the front rows of seats were only for white people. If the white people's seats were full, the driver could move the sign for the 'coloured section' back so that black people had to get out of their seats to make room for white people coming on. Black people were not allowed to walk through the section where the white people were sitting. They had to pay their fare at the front and then get off the bus and walk to the back door, but if the bus moved off before they could get back on, they had to walk, even though they had paid their fare.

Journalist   Did you go to school eventually, Rosa?

Old Rosa   Oh yes. I went to the Industrial School for Girls in Montgomery and then I went on to the Laboratory School run by the Teachers' College for Negroes. But I didn't finish school then.

Young Rosa   *(Coming in from school, Rosa looks about 12 now)*
Mummy you look ill. What's wrong?

Leona	I'm too ill to look after Grandma. I need to stay in bed for most of each day. I'm sorry Rosa. You will have to leave school and stay at home to look after us and do the housework.
(Exit Leona)	
Journalist	And so your school days ended.
Old Rosa	For a while. I got married young. In 1932 I married Raymond Parks. He was a barber in Montgomery. *(Enter Raymond)*
Raymond	*(to Young Rosa, who looks 19)* You know Rosa, I really think you should go back to school and get your High School Diploma. You're a smart lady and it's a waste of your brains for you not to finish school off properly.
N	A year later in 1933.
Raymond	You've passed your High School Diploma, congratulations. You know, Rosa, less than 7% of African Americans have passed it. *(They exit.)*
Old Rosa	I also had a job as a domestic worker and an aide in a hospital.
Journalist	Were you allowed to vote?
Old Rosa	Eventually. I applied three times before I was finally allowed to register.
Journalist	What else did you do?
Old Rosa	I kept on going to church. I have belonged to the African Methodist Church all my life. Raymond and I both belonged to the Civil Rights Movement and I became its secretary. I was the only woman there at the time.
Journalist	Tell me about your argument on the bus.

(About sixteen white children walk onto the stage, each carrying a chair. They set their chairs down in four rows of four with an aisle up the middle, most of them sitting down. James Blake carries on his chair and sits at the front as the driver.)

Old Rosa	It really began in 1943, when I was thirty years old. It was a rainy day. The bus driver was a man called James Blake.

(Young Rosa steps onto the bus and pays her fare to the driver. Behind are four rows of white people sitting. There is an empty chair next to the 'door'.)

Blake	You can't walk past these people. Go outside the bus and walk to the end and come in through the back door.
Old Rosa	I dropped my purse and sat down on a white person's chair to pick it up.

(Young Rosa mimes the action.)

Blake	Get off that chair! That's for white people, not for you!

(Rosa gets off the bus. Everyone lifts their chair and moves off stage to symbolize the bus moving off.)

Old Rosa	As soon as I stepped off the bus, he drove off at once knowing that I didn't have time to get on at the back, even though I had paid my fare. I had to walk five miles home in the rain. I did a lot of walking in Montgomery when I was young. I wanted to avoid the humiliation of being treated like a second-class citizen. It was twelve years later in 1955 when I made history on the bus. I got on the bus on 1st December 1955 and paid my fare. The driver was that James Blake, the same driver

as in 1943. I walked past lots of empty seats for white people and sat in the coloured section.

(Children carry their chairs back on to form the bus rows as before. They leave the chairs empty and exit. Rosa [now 42] pays her fare and walks up the aisle into the black section.)

Old Rosa   A few stops later, lots of white people got on the bus.

(White children enter and fill up all the rows in front of Rosa.)

Blake   You black people get off those seats and let the white people sit down.

(Three black people, sitting near Rosa, stand up and move back up the bus. Rosa stays in her seat.)

Blake   You'd better shift yourself and let me have that seat.

Rosa   No!

Blake   Why don't you get out of that seat?

Rosa   I don't think I should have to get out of it!

Blake   If you don't get out of that seat, I shall call the police and have you arrested.

Rosa   That's fine. Do that.

Blake   Police! Police! Arrest this black woman. She is refusing to get off the seat for a white woman.   *(Enter policeman.)*

Rosa   Why do you push us around?

Policeman   The law is the law and you're under arrest for not obeying the law.

(Children move the chairs offstage. Enter magistrate.)

Magistrate   You are found guilty of refusing to get off a seat on a bus to give it to a white person. You are fined ten dollars and four dollars court costs.

(They exit.)

Journalist   What made you refuse to give up your seat, Rosa? Were you tired?

Old Rosa   No I wasn't tired in the least. The only thing I was tired of was us black people giving in to those laws instead of standing up to them. But we didn't let the matter rest there. Soon a group of black American leaders got together to form a pressure group to protest against the segregation laws.

(Enter a group of black people including Rosa, Raymond, Rev Abernathy, Dr Martin Luther King.)

Rev Abernathy

I reckon this is as good a time as any to make a stand against the segregation laws. With Rosa in the news, we must use the publicity opportunity to bring everyone's attention to our cause.

Person in the group

It's time to let them know we are prepared to fight.

Martin Luther King

Now wait a minute, we have got to go about this in a peaceful manner. If we become violent, we will destroy any sympathy we have for our cause. Remember Mahatma Gandhi, he brought about great change without violence. I believe the more peacefully we protest the sooner we will bring about change.

Rev Abernathy
I agree. We must make this a respectable organization. I think we should call it the 'Montgomery Improvement Association'.

People in the group
Good idea. / I agree. / That's a good idea.

Rev Abernathy
Now we must have a leader and make some decisions. I suggest Dr Martin Luther King as our leader. Those who agree, raise your hand.

(Everyone raises a hand)

Martin Luther King
Thank you everyone. Now I think we must get a protest started quickly. I reckon the best peaceful protest would be for all black people in Montgomery to stop using the public bus service. It's peaceful, it's legal and the bus company will lose hundreds of dollars.

People in the crowd
Great idea. / That'll show we have some power. / We should do it. / That'll do more good than fighting.

Martin Luther King   Those in favour, raise your hand.

(Everyone raises a hand)

Martin Luther King
That's great, we'll start at once. We must get the word round to the whole Negro population. I shall need a secretary. Mrs Parks, would you be my secretary?

Rosa   Er... yes, I'd be glad to.

Martin Luther King
That's great. We must act at once. We will put posters in all the black churches. We must make thousands of leaflets and give them out to the black people, and put an advertisement in the front of the Montgomery Advertiser asking black people to stay away from the buses. We must be prepared to keep up the boycott until they agree to hire black drivers and all seats are for the use of black and white people equally.

(They exit)

Journalist   How long did you keep it up, Rosa?

Old Rosa   Just over a year. The following year in November, The Supreme Court outlawed separating black and white people on buses and the order reached Montgomery just before Christmas, so we called off our protest and started using the buses again.

Journalist   So that solved that problem.

Old Rosa   Not completely. I lost my job in a department store and Raymond decided to leave his, after his boss forbade him to talk about me or the case. Some white people couldn't stand our winning the fight. They attacked Martin Luther King's home and threw bombs into churches and homes of black church ministers. We moved to Hampton. I found a job as a hostess in a hotel and later I worked as a seamstress. In 1965, I got a job as a secretary and receptionist for a member of the House of Representatives in Detroit and I worked there until I retired.

Journalist   What else did you do?

Old Rosa Raymond died in 1977 and my friend Elaine Eason Steele and I founded the Rosa and Raymond Parks Institute for Self Development in 1987. Right now I'm just working on this book, Rosa Parks: My Story.

Journalist It looks like it's going to be a mighty fine book, Rosa. I wish you a lot of luck with it.

Old Rosa Well thank you.

(They shake hands, stand up and exit.)

N After Rosa retired, she was given several awards and prizes. On September 9th 1994, President Bill Clinton presented Rosa with the Presidential Medal of Freedom. Time magazine named her one of the most influential people of the twentieth century.

N Rosa Parks died on 24th October 2005. In Montgomery and Detroit the buses had black ribbons on the front seats until after her funeral.

N Condoleeza Rice a Government Secretary of State said at her funeral that if it hadn't been for Rosa's courage in standing up to unjust laws, she might never have become a Secretary of State.

N Let us pray.
Oh God. Thank you for the life of Rosa Parks. Help us always to stand up for what is right. Help us to remember that we are more able to change things by behaving peacefully.

Chapter 1 Black & Asian history assemblies

Mahatma Gandhi

1869 – 1948

Mahatma Gandhi is one of the most revered people of the twentieth century. In India he is commemorated on 2nd October which was his birthday. This script reviews a selection of the events of his life.

> **Characters**
>
> Gandhi
> Gandhi's father
> Gandhi's mother
> Kasturba, his wife
> Magistrate
> Ticket collector
> Clerk
> A friend
> Judge
> A few poor farmers
> President Nehru
> People in the crowd
> Lots of narrators

(The class are on stage in an arc at the back. They step forward to play their part.)

N Good morning and welcome to our assembly. Our class would like to tell you about Mahatma Gandhi. He was a Hindu leader who led his people to oppose unfair laws and to get Independence from Britain for India.

N When he was born, his name was Mohondas Karamchand Gandhi. He was born in Porbandar in Gujarat on 2nd October 1869. His father was a diwan or chief minister of the town. This means that Mohondas was born into the Vaishyas or third class of the caste system.

N What is a caste system?

N In India, at that time, there was a caste system which had lasted for at least two thousand years. Their whole race was divided into five castes or classes. The top one was the Brahmins who were priests and scholars. The second were the Kshatriyas, the warriors and rulers. Third were Vaishayas the traders and merchants and fourth were the Shudras who were labourers and servants. At the bottom of the system were the Untouchables who did the worst jobs like cleaning toilets. You could not get out of your caste and you were only allowed to do the jobs of that caste and marry people of the same caste. Gandhi hated the caste system because it was so unfair.

Gandhi's mother
Remember, Mohondas, it is important never to harm anyone else or any living creature. A good Hindu always respects people of every other race and religion in the world. You only eat vegetarian food and it is important to fast occasionally to drive impurities from the body. Remember this always.

Gandhi Yes, Mother, I will.

Gandhi's father
And now, Mohandas, we have some good news for you. We have spoken to our friends, the Makhanjis. They have a lovely daughter called Kasturba. So we have arranged for you to marry her. Now that you are thirteen we think you are old enough. We will, of course, allow you to meet her before you are married.

Gandhi Oh. Thank you father.

(Kasturba enters stage and walks up to Gandhi. They smile at each other.)

N And so Gandhi was married. This did not stop him going to school and college. He went to university in Bombay, as his father wanted him to be a barrister. He did not like it much but he leapt at the opportunity to go to London University the month before his nineteenth birthday.

N When he got to England, he studied English customs and other religions like Christianity, Judaism, Buddhism, Sikhism and Islam.

N He returned to India to work as a lawyer, but he did not have much luck and so in 1893, Gandhi set off for Natal in South Africa to work for an Indian company for a year. Here he encountered racial prejudice for the first time.

(A court scene)

Magistrate *(looking at Gandhi with disapproval)*
Remove that turban!

Gandhi Why?

Magistrate This is South Africa. You do not dress like that here.

Gandhi I have every right to wear my turban.

Magistrate No you haven't. Take it off or leave at once.

Gandhi I'm not staying here. *(He storms off in disgust)*

N Gandhi found racial prejudice everywhere. One day on a train...

(Ticket collector enters and sees Gandhi sitting on a seat.)

Ticket collector
What are you doing here?

Gandhi I am travelling to Natal. Here is my ticket.

Ticket collector
You're not allowed in first class.

Gandhi Why not? I have paid my fare.

Ticket collector
Black people are not allowed in first class. Go down to third class with the rest of the blacks.

Gandhi	No! I have paid my fare. I am not hurting anyone else. I am staying here.

(Two ticket collectors grab Gandhi, taking an arm each and pulling him off the stage.)

N	It was hard to get hotel rooms if you were black.

(A hotel reception. Gandhi enters)

Gandhi	I would like a room please.

Clerk	No, we're full.

(He turns to go and a white person comes in.)

Man	I would like a room, please.

Clerk	Certainly, sir. I can give you a comfortable room with a view.

N	Near the end of his year in South Africa, Gandhi was reading a newspaper one day.

Gandhi	*(Reading)*
Look at this! The Government has passed a law saying that Indians are not allowed to vote.

N	Gandhi and his friends protested. They started an organization called the Natal Indian Congress in 1894. They got the Indians in South Africa to act as one group of people, without their caste system, working together as a group to fight racism. Then the South African War started.

Gandhi	*(Addressing the crowd)*
This is our chance to show everyone that we can be full citizens of South Africa. Let us get together and form a voluntary ambulance organization. We will pick up the wounded and take them to hospitals and treat wounded people as well as we can. If we show that we are able to play our part in being good citizens, surely they will give all Indians full citizenship when the war is over.

N	Gandhi and the other Indians spent the war years working to support South Africa, but it did not help them to gain full citizens' rights. In fact after the war, things got worse for the Indians.

Gandhi	*(Addressing a crowd)*
The South African Government has passed a law that all Indians have to register and carry identity cards. We will stand up to them, but we will do it peacefully. We will not obey this law. We will have peaceful protests but when the police come for us, we will never fight back. We will never use violence, even when they use it against us.

N	For seven years, Gandhi and his supporters disobeyed the law. They refused to go to the registry offices and when identity cards were forced on them, they got together and burnt them in public. There were beaten and put in prison. The government was criticized heavily for using such dreadful punishments against people who were protesting peacefully. At last the government had to give in.

N	Gandhi returned to India and soon took up the case of the poor. He visited the poor farmers in Champaram and Kheda.

Gandhi	*(To a group of farmers who are weak with hunger)*
What is wrong?

Farmer	We are starving. The British landlords forced us to grow indigo and won't allow us to grow food. We are becoming ill and we cannot feed our children. And now they are demanding a tax which we cannot possibly pay.

N Gandhi organized lots of his supporters and volunteers to come to the villages to help the people, bringing them food to get back to health. He also organized peaceful protests and at last the British landlords had to allow the farmers to grow. At this time the Indians began to call him 'Mahatma' which means a revered person and 'Bapu' which means father.

Gandhi *(Addressing the class who form the crowd, reading if necessary.)*
We must persuade the British to leave India, but we must do it by peaceful means. There are causes for which I am prepared to die, but there is no cause, for which I am prepared to kill. We must never use violence. We must be a race of people who are all working together, rich and poor, men and women, people of all castes. We will disobey their laws and when they punish us, we will not fight back even if they are violent towards us. We will only buy food and materials which are made in India. We must never buy anything which is British made. We should spend a little time each day spinning our own cloth to make our own clothes. We must not go into British educational buildings or law courts. If anyone has a job working for the British Government, I ask you to leave it now. Let the British see that we will have nothing to do with them so they cannot possibly govern us. In the end by protesting peacefully, we will win and the British will have to go home.

(Crowd cheers)

N The Indians all joined in their campaign of peaceful disobedience. Occasionally there was violence and Gandhi, frightened that all his work would be undone, called off the campaign. The British thought him a trouble-maker and in 1922 they called him to court for sedition. That means persuading people to rebel against the government.

(Enter Judge and Gandhi)

Judge You have been found guilty of urging people to rebel against the state. I sentence you to six years in prison.

(Gandhi is taken away)

N Gandhi only spent two years in prison and when he came out, he spent a few years working to fight poverty, alcoholism and putting an end to the caste system. In 1928, he called on the British Government to get out of India or face a new campaign of civil disobedience from the Indians. The British did not answer, so Gandhi's party the Indian National Congress unfurled a flag of India in Lahore and declared Indian Independence. They then had a long protest march to the sea to protest against the British putting a tax on salt. As a result over 60,000 Indians were imprisoned.

N The British began to realize that they would not have any peace until they sat down with the Indians and made an agreement. Unfortunately the Indians did not get everything that Gandhi wanted and so the fighting went on. The protests often became violent although Gandhi was always opposed to violence.

(Enter Ghandi's friend)

Friend of Gandhi
Bapu, how can you be so opposed to people fighting to protect themselves. All we are doing is standing up for ourselves.

Gandhi When I despair, I remember that all through history the way of truth and love has

	always won. There have been tyrants and murderers and for a time they seem unbeatable, but in the end they always fall.
Friend of Gandhi	But Bapu, our people have been treated so cruelly by the British. Surely we cannot be blamed for wanting to have our own back.
Gandhi	An eye for an eye makes the whole world blind.
N	At the end of the 2nd World War, the British Government gave permission for India to become completely independent from Britain. Gandhi was pleased that the British had handed over power to the Indians but he was sad that India was divided in India and Pakistan.
N	On 30th January 1948, while on his way to the Mandir, Gandhi was shot and killed. President Nehru spoke of him on the radio.
Nehru	Friends and comrades, the light has gone out of our lives and there is darkness everywhere, and I do not know how to say it. Our dear leader, Bapu, as we called him, the father of the nation, is dead. We will never see him again. We will never again run to him for advice or comfort and that is a terrible blow for me and millions and millions in our country.
N	Let us pray. Oh God, help us always to try to live our lives in a peaceful way. Help us to learn to sort out our quarrels with persuasion and without fighting.

Chapter 2 Buddhist assembly

Buddha Day

The first full moon in May

There are over 400 million Buddhists in the world. Though concentrated in South East Asia, there are still over 5,000 in Britain. Buddhism is a religion of care for other people and creatures and worthy to be presented in a multi-cultural society. The Buddha's riches-to-rags story if presented sympathetically is inspiring to children of all faiths.

> **Characters**
>
> Prince Siddhartha/the Buddha
> King Suddhodana, his father
> Queen Maya, his mother
> Siddhartha's wife
> Servant
> 2 astrologers
> People at the christening party
> Old man
> Old woman with her children around her
> Group of people looking sad
> Dancing girls
> Lots of narrators

N   Welcome to our assembly. This month on 2nd May, Buddhists celebrate Buddha day.

N   Who was the Buddha? Is he a God?

N   No. He was a very wise man who lived two thousand, five hundred years ago. Today Buddhists follow his way of life all over the world, but mainly in Asia.

N   Let us tell you the story of his life.

N   Two thousand five hundred years ago,
Where the mountain peaks were topped with snow.
And the trees on the mountain sides grew tall
In a land which we now call Nepal.

(Enter King Suddhodana and his wife, looking at each other in a kindly way, arms linked.)

N   King Suddhodana governed a small nation.
They were a very mixed population.
There were people who were ill and those in health
And some in poverty next to some in wealth.

N   Now King Suddhodana and his wife
Lived in their palace, a comfortable life.
Queen Maya, one day, was over the moon.

Maya My dearest, I'll be having a baby soon.

Suddhodana This is wonderful news. I'm delighted, my dear.
I can hardly wait 'til our baby is here.

Maya Last night, my dear, I'd a marvellous dream.
I saw a white elephant happily walking.
Our baby will be special. That's a clear sign.
He will be a great ruler, wise and benign.

(Exit Maya and then re-enters carrying a doll, and looking thrilled. Play any happy oriental music softly in the background. All of the rest of the class move around happily chatting and admiring the baby. Two astrologers at the front look on thoughtfully. Pupils must speak up loudly and clearly above the music.)

N And on the day of their prince's birth
The entire palace rang with mirth.
All around sprang up pretty flowers.
Out of season rain fell in showers.
Scent and music filled the air for hours.

N Wise astrologers watched the party. And saw the King all happy and hearty.

(Astrologers approach the king. Music fades away.)

1st astrologer
We have seen it in the stars, Suddhodana.
One day this child will be a man.
When that happens he will either be
A king of power and majesty,
Ruling over kingdoms, strongly and wisely.

2nd astrologer
Or, if not, he may choose
To become a monk and lose
All this comfort and start teaching
And spend his life in poverty, preaching.

N Now King Suddhodana didn't like it much,
The thought of his son leaving such
A happy, loving comfortable home
Among the poor and ill to roam.

Suddhodana
How can I prevent this from happening?
Come, give good advice to your King.

1st astrologer
If your son stays in the palace grounds
Unaware of the world that surrounds.
Knowing nothing of illness and pain,
Old age or death, then he will reign
In this kingdom and far beyond
And be a great leader his whole life long.

2nd astrologer
But if he goes beyond the palace walls
He will see sights that distress and appall.

>If he sees poverty, death and disease,
>Those awful sights will release
>A flow of sympathy from his heart
>And he will straightaway depart
>From this palace and leave his wife
>Searching a completely different life.

Suddhodana *(horrified)*
>I could not bear it. It must never be.
>We must keep him here living comfortably.

(The party group move to the rear of the stage and Maya walks off carrying her doll.)

N
>The happy pair called their prince Siddhartha.
>A week later the king was broken-hearted.
>Queen Maya died and her sister became
>The prince's mother in all but name.

(Siddhartha enters and walks to the king, who hugs him.)

N
>The years passed and the happy prince grew.
>Surrounded by comfort, he never knew
>There could be nasty things in life.
>And so in bliss he took a wife.

(Enter Siddhartha's wife. She links arms with him and they begin walking in a leisurely manner round the stage admiring the garden.)

N
>The couple lived in a palace of high walls.
>With gardens and fountains and magnificent halls.
>They had plenty of food and servants galore,
>But strangely Siddhartha wanted more.

(Enter servant, exit wife.)

Siddhartha
>Why am I constantly kept in here?
>Why does my father always fear
>To let me go out of the palace to see
>What is out there? It is time I was free.

N
>No one dared to disobey the king.
>So Siddhartha grew, knowing nothing.
>He had a son now and he was eager to go
>Outside the walls but the king said no.

(Siddhartha and servant mime getting into a chariot and going for a ride. Enter an old man who sits alone at the side of the stage, an old woman who sits on the stage with her children round her and a group of people looking distressed stand at the other side of the stage.)

N
>Eventually one day Siddhartha convinced
>A loyal servant to obey his prince
>And take him on a chariot outside
>The palace grounds for a little ride.
>And the sights that he saw left him horrified.

Siddhartha *(Looking at an old man)*
>Why is that man, all weak and tired?

Servant	He is old and frail and should be retired. He has no children to attend to his needs So he has to beg by the roadside and weeds.
Siddhartha	*(Looking at a woman with her children round her)* Why is that person over there being carried? Why does she look so anxious and harried?
Servant	She's incurably ill. She'll never recover. Those children have to look after their mother.
Siddhartha	Those people over there looking dreadfully sad. They're crying so hard. What can be so bad?
Servant	Their father has died. They'll never see him again.
Siddhartha	Can it really be that life comes to an end?
Servant	My prince. You've been shielded from all of life's ills. Your father forbade it. He wants you still To remain in ignorance and absolute bliss. He's determined you'll never find out about this.
Siddhartha	Over there is a man in a saffron gown. With a contented expression walking around.
Servant	That man is a monk. He has no luxury. He works and prays in a monastery.
N	And so our prince became aware That death and illness happened everywhere.

(Siddhartha and his servant mime getting into the chariot and returning home.)

N	So Siddhartha returned home, changed. All the comfort seemed so strange. How could he live in such luxury While so many others lived in poverty.
N	Knowing all this made the prince grieve. And so he decided it was time to leave His beautiful palace and live with the poor.

(King comes on stage. Siddhartha approaches the king and mimes speaking to him.)

Suddhodana	But why, my son, what are you going for?
Siddhartha	Father it's wrong that I should live In luxury. I'm so rich I should give Something to the poor to ease their pain How can they bear all that stress and strain?

(Siddhartha takes leave of his wife and son who cry as he leaves. He approaches some men and mimes speaking to them.)

N	Siddhartha kissed his wife and son good-bye And left his home with his friends to try A less comfortable life. He went to some caves And there some old people gave Him advice to live without enough food. But all that hardship did no good.

(Siddhartha sits looking unhappy, watching girls who mime dancing and singing and move on.)

N	One day in thought he was sitting Along came dancing girls, happily singing. They were joyful and lively and full of vitality, The merriest girls in the locality.
Siddhartha	They've got it right. Now I must find How to have a calm and peaceful mind. I shall sit under this bodhi tree. I'm staying here until I can see How to live in complete contentment.
N	At last he received enlightenment.

(Child sets some large lotus flowers cut out of sugar paper on the floor.)

Siddhartha	The way to live in untroubled peace Is to be at all times released From poisons of ignorance, hatred and greed. A different life I shall now lead.
N	And looking over the pool he noticed The pretty buds and flowers of lotus.

(Siddartha picks up a lotus flower.)

Siddhartha	The full lotus flower is like someone Who has thought hard and become Fully enlightened. And so the plant became A symbol of a person who has attained The state of true enlightenment And able to live in pure contentment.
N	That's a wonderful story. What did Siddhartha do then?
N	He gave his first sermon in the deer park in Sarnath in India. He spent the rest of his life preaching to others about his beliefs. From then on he was called the Buddha which means 'enlightened one'. He lived until he was about eighty.
N	What do Buddhists believe?
N	They do not believe that the Buddha was a God. He did not want to be a God, but he did want to show people how to live a contented, satisfying life. He believed that you should not try to live in either great luxury or hardship. It is sensible to take a Middle Path between the two extremes.
N	Buddhists strive to be enlightened like the Buddha. This means that they must meditate to be able to think clearly and drive all thought of hatred and greed out of their lives and so have peace of mind and contentment.
N	The three jewels of Buddhism are 1 – the Buddha 2 – his teaching 3 – the Buddhist community.
N	They have a set of guidelines called the Five Precepts 1 – You must not hurt or harm any person or animal. 2 – You must not steal. 3 – You must have a sensible way of life.

4 – You must not speak unkindly or tell lies.
5 – You should not take drugs or alcohol.

N Let us pray.
Oh God, whichever religion we follow, help us to value the teachings of the wise Buddha. Help us to be honest and to treat others with respect and kindness. Please help us to remember that we can have more pleasure by being kind to others than by gaining a lot of possessions.

Chapter 3 Chinese assemblies

Yuan Tan

(Chinese New Year) January/February

Even if you have only a few Chinese children in the school, they will all find the story behind the Chinese zodiac fun to present. The New Year normally falls in January or February.

> **Characters**
>
> The Emperor of Jade
> Rat
> Cat
> Ox
> Tiger
> Rabbit
> Dragon
> Snake
> Horse
> Goat
> Monkey
> Rooster
> Dog
> Pig (Each child can wear a mask for their part)*
> Emperor's messenger
> Narrators
> * Educational Printing Services Limited publishes 'Book of Masks' which contains many animal masks

N	Good morning and welcome to our assembly. This week, Chinese people across the world are celebrating the Chinese New Year. It always falls in either January or February. This year, 2007, is 4704 in the Chinese calendar. (Change the numbers as appropriate.)

N	Every year Chinese people celebrate the New Year with parties, cards and gifts, and children get money in red envelopes.

N	Long ago in Ancient China, people had no way of knowing how many years had passed or how they could record them. Our class would like to tell you the legend behind the naming of the years in the Chinese Zodiac.

Emperor of Jade *(Addressing everyone except the animals)*
>	The seasons come and the years go.
>	They are passing quickly and we do not know
>	How many years have come and gone
>	Or how many years the world will go on.

(Emperor moves away, in thought)

N He was so interested, he spent his leisure
Thinking up a way to measure
And name the years as they passed.
Another new year was approaching fast.

Emperor *(Returning to the group)*
Gather round, I have worked it out at last.
Send messages out across the entire
Land to each animal in the Empire.
Tell every creature there'll be a race
At a specially chosen place.
It'll be a straight part of the river bank
And every animal of every rank
Will come together at the chosen time
Along the bank, in a straight line.
I'll choose a place where the river is wide
And they can race to the other side.
As each one reaches the opposite bank,
We'll line them up in order and rank
And name our years after the winners.
That's the prize for the best twelve swimmers.

N And so they sent out a proclamation
Across the entire Chinese nation.

(People move back and the creatures, in masks, enter.)

Emperor's messenger
Gather round, all you animals with ambition.
The Emperor's having a competition.
If you want some glory and fame
The first twelve of you will have your name
Honoured forever and for all time.
Just go to the river and get into line.
When the signal is given you fly or swim
To the other side, and if you win
You'll go into the Chinese zodiac
And every twelve years the people will track
The order in which you finished the race.
Now line up everyone! Find a space!

N All the animals gathered in a throng.
Excited and eager they bunched along
The whole river bank in a noisy flurry.
They bumped and shuffled in a hurry-scurry.
They irritated and argued and squabbled,
And pushed and shoved and staggered and wobbled.

(All the creatures in a disorderly bunch, bumping and pushing. They must mime trying not to actually touch each other.)

Monkey A year should be named after me
Because I'm clever

N	boasted Monkey.
Ox	That's not always clear to me. In fact I think you're rather cheeky.
Horse	I'm much stronger than you, of course. A year should be mine,
N	answered Horse. Goat hated to hear them rudely calling out Insults, and naughty creatures falling out. He leapt up onto a rock and frowned At all the creatures on the ground.

(Goat jumps up and wags his finger)

Goat	Let's not argue. Make amends. Now all shake hands and let's be friends. I'm sure all this can be resolved If all the creatures who are involved Just behave sensibly and show goodwill.
N	But the animals went on arguing still.
Rooster	*(to Rabbit)* I really don't know why you're trying. You can't fly or swim. You'll be crying Out for help when we're all finishing You'll be sinking and probably wishing You'd stayed at home all safe and sound. Silly rabbit, you'll be drowned.
Rabbit	*(shyly)* You are always saying something nasty. Why are you so horrid to me?
Rat	I think this race is rather unfair Because it's in a river where Not all of us can move with ease. Ox, can I jump onto your back please?
Ox	Of course, my friend, you are so light I won't notice you, so that's all right.
Cat	May I come too? I'll be no trouble.
N	And Cat leapt on, at the double.

(They both stay close to the Ox one on either side)

Snake	Unfortunately I'm not a sswimmer, But that won't sstop me being a winner. I'll sslither round Horsse's leg And ass long ass I can keep my head Above the water I will make it. I don't know how old Horsse will take it. He'll be sswimming so eagerly With luck he will not noticce me.

(Snake stands closely by Horse)

Tiger	I'm not sure if I can do it.

Dragon	Just concentrate and you'll get through it.

Dog	I'm worried too. I can't swim that length.

Pig	Yes you can. Use all your strength.

N	So the animals lined up at the edge of the river,
Trembling with excitement and all in a quiver.
Raring to go and desperate to win.
Those who could fly or paddle or swim.
Bustling and hustling all in a row.
All except tired and hungry Boar.
He gobbled a meal and began to snore.

(Except Pig, Monkey, Rooster and Goat, who are at the side of the stage, the creatures all line up in a row, well spread out and jump, move their arms and legs 'swimming' on the spot, pushing, shoving, elbowing.)

Emperor's Messenger
	On your marks get ready, get set and go!

N	A mile-long splash rose into the air
As the arms and legs scrambled everywhere.
And miaous and squeaks and barks and bellows
Pierced the air as browns and yellows
And greens and greys and whites and blues
Of feathers and fur and hair and scales
Mingled and mangled in howls and wails.

N	The creatures cheered and snuffled and choked.
They hissed and clamoured and gasped and croaked.
They pushed and shoved and elbowed and kicked.
They helped and hindered and carried and tricked.
Some flew, some waded, some floated, some sank
Some were exhausted and stopped and drank.
As each kept an eye on the opposite bank.

(10 seconds of each creature making the appropriate noise)

N	All the commotion woke the sleeping boar.
Although he was sleepy he quietly swore
He would not be left out of the fun
And into the river he started to run.

(Pig mimes the above)

N	Goat and Monkey and Rooster found
A raft abandoned on the ground
Near the river bank covered in weeds.

(They walk along the stage and find an imaginary raft.)

Goat	A little clean is all this needs.

N	And soon the trio were all aboard

　　　　　　　Paddling fast to the opposite shore.
　　　　　　　Off went Rabbit with a skip and a jog
　　　　　　　On stepping stones till he found a log
　　　　　　　And leapt up onto it and went for a ride
　　　　　　　And paddled his way to the other side.
　　　　　　　Along came Dragon gliding above.

(Rabbit bunny-hops on the spot and leaps onto the log.)

Dragon　　　You're struggling Rabbit. Would you like a shove?

Rabbit　　　Oh thank you, Dragon,

N　　　　　called Rabbit with a shout.
　　　　　　　Dragon drew breath and blew it out
　　　　　　　At the back of the log and it gathered pace
　　　　　　　And lucky old Rabbit was back in the race.

(Dragon comes to her and puffs behind her.)

N　　　　　Dog loved the water, he splashed and played
　　　　　　　Enjoyed himself but was delayed
　　　　　　　With bathing, cavorting and having fun
　　　　　　　'Til he saw that the race was almost won.

(Dog playing in the water)

N　　　　　And as they neared the end of the race,
　　　　　　　Rat behaved with a very bad grace.
　　　　　　　Safe and secure on Ox's back,
　　　　　　　He crept up behind the unlucky Cat.
　　　　　　　And pushed her into the flowing river.
　　　　　　　She was shocked and hurt and all in a shiver.
　　　　　　　And as if that was not treacherous enough.

(Rats pushes Cat over and she leaves the stage, in disgust.)

N　　　　　And when Ox was almost out of puff,
　　　　　　　Rat stepped slyly over Ox's head,
　　　　　　　Leapt onto the bank and won instead
　　　　　　　Of the kind-hearted Ox who had carried him.

(Rat rushes ahead of Ox and up to the Emperor. The rest of the creatures go to the Emperor in turn and he lines them up in the correct order.)

Ox　　　　　That's not fair!

N　　　　　The poor Ox harried him.
　　　　　　　And next came Tiger, exhausted and drained.

Tiger　　　I shall never swim that river again.

N　　　　　And just as the tiger staggered and flopped,
　　　　　　　Off his log to the bank, the rabbit hopped.

Rabbit　　　I'd never have done it without my friend.
　　　　　　　Good old Dragon blew me to the end.

N　　　　　And Dragon of course flew in just after,

	Followed by Snake curled up with laughter. He unwound himself from Horse's limb Leapt over his back in front of him.
Snake	I've beaten you, Horse, but thanks for the lift.
N	Horse turned away in disgust, quite miffed. The raft drifted in to the place at length Goat, Monkey and Rooster were eighth, ninth and tenth;
N	And Dog doggie-paddled at last to the shore And was closely followed by the lively Boar. And poor old Cat all shivery and cross Never forgave the rat for her loss. That's the reason why, to this day, Cats eat rats or they drive them away.
Emperor	Well done, winners, you'll be celebrated. Each year one of you will be fêted As each year will be dedicated To each one of you for the rest of time.

(All the creatures clap and cheer.)

N	Every year, Chinese people celebrate the new year with parties and cards and gifts and children get money in red envelopes.
N	People say that we resemble the animal in whose year we were born. We would like to tell you about the people who were born in each year.

(The dates given are for the time of writing, 2006. The date in brackets is for the next date. Obviously teachers can select the appropriate one.)

Rat	The last year of the Rat began on 19th February 1996 (7th February 2008). Rats are clever and have a great imagination. They work hard and would like to do well but do not always manage it because they are not confident or well-organized. Their family and friends love them because they are kind and loyal to them.
Ox	The last year of the Ox began on 7th February 1997. (26th January 2009). Oxen are strong, reliable people and are often the ones who take charge of the group. They work hard and are often successful. They are patient and loyal, good at making friends and keeping them.
Tiger	The last year of the Tiger began on 28th January 1998 (14th February 2010). Tigers are loving and sympathetic people. They are self-assured and want to do things their own way but are not always able to cope with difficulties. They turn to their friends for comfort when things are not going well for them.
Rabbit	The last year of the Rabbit began on February 16th 1999 (February 3rd 2011). Rabbits are loving and take care of their families. They don't like arguments and are a little shy. They love having fun.
Dragon	The last year of the Dragon began on 5th February 2000 (23rd January 2012). Dragons are self-assured and ambitious. They are lively and bring out the best in other people and so they are popular. Dragons love having fun and enjoy doing lots of different things. Everyone loves them because they encourage others to do lots of things. This is the only make-believe creature in the Chinese zodiac.
Snake	The last year of the Snake was on 24th January 2001 (10th February 2013). Snakes

	are perfectionists. They are clever especially at business. They are independent and kindly spoken.
Horse	The last year of the Horse began on 12th February 2002 (31st January 2014). Horses are romantic creatures who are determined to do well and never leave a job unfinished. They can handle a large amount of work on their own.
Goat	The last year of the Goat began on 1st February 2003 (19th February 2015). Goats are graceful, artistic and kind. They are peace-loving and eager to avoid conflict. Although they are gentle they are good at standing up to people who would take advantage of them.
Monkey	The last year of the Monkey began on 22nd January 2004 (8th February 2016). Monkeys are naughty but intelligent people. They are popular and tend to get on in life because they are good at sorting out problems and getting out of difficulties.
Rooster	The last year of the Rooster began on 9th February 2005 (28th January 2017). Roosters are hard-working, determined and self-assured people. They are punctual and efficient and like having everyone's attention. They love compliments but although they hate criticism they are quick to criticize others.
Dog	The last year of the Dog began on 29th January 2006 (16th February 2018). Dogs are loyal, trustworthy helpful and fair-minded. They are good listeners and respected by others but tend to be anxious and rather unforgiving.
Pig	The last year of the Pig began on 18th February 2007 (February 5th 2019). Pigs are calm, level-headed people. They love having fun and are willing to share with their friends. They are trustworthy but rather untidy.
N	Let us pray. Oh God, thank you for the company of friends and family. Help us always to be willing to help others and to treat others fairly.

Emperor of Jade
    We hope you have enjoyed our assembly and we wish you all a Happy New Year.

Chapter 3 Chinese assemblies

Dragon Boat Festival

May/June

This is one of the three most important festivals in the Chinese calendar and it is the one which has been celebrated for the longest time.

> **Characters**
>
> The Chinese Emperor, Hue
> Qu Yuan, one of the Emperor's ministers
> 1st Minister
> 2nd Minister
> Waiter
> 1st Fisherman
> 2nd Fisherman
> 1st Woman
> 2nd Woman
> Lots of narrators

N   Good morning and welcome to our assembly. This month the Chinese people will be celebrating the Dragon Boat Festival.

N   It is one of the most important Chinese festivals and it is the oldest one. It has been celebrated every year since hundreds of years before Christ.

N   The Dragon Boat festival is celebrated on the fifth day of the fifth lunar month of the Chinese calendar every year. It is sometimes known as the Double Fifth Day. It normally falls in May or June.

N   It is a very lively and colourful celebration with dragon boats racing and people eating zongzi and drinking wine.

N   Why the fifth day of the fifth month?

N   Long ago people thought that the fifth month of the Chinese calendar was unlucky and the fifth day was an especially bad day. So one of the aims of the festival was to drive away evil and bring them some luck. Dragons are a sign of good luck to the Chinese.

N   There are lots of traditions about the Chinese Boat festival. We would like to tell you some of them.

N   One tradition of the festival is to have races in dragon boats. The race symbolizes a fight among the dragons and is supposed to bring about rain, which people needed to make their crops grow.

N   The dragon boats are brightly painted and decorated. They have a dragon carved into the wood at the front and before the race they have a ceremony of painting the dragon's eyes to bring it to life.

(Show a picture of a dragon boat, either a painted one, a picture on an overhead projector sheet or on PowerPoint.)

N	At the front of every boat there must be a drummer and a flag catcher. The drummer pounds the rhythm for the oarsmen to row the boat. The flag-catcher must grab the flag at the end of the race for his team to win. At the back of the dragon boat they paint brightly coloured dragon scales.
N	It is a very exciting event and is held all over China, Hong Kong, Taiwan and other Chinese countries.
N	Another aim of the festival is to drive away evil spirits before the summer because this is the time when people most often fall ill. Sometimes Chinese people hang a picture of Zhong Kui on their door to drive away evil spirits. Some people drink Xiong Huang wine to keep evil spirits away and children carry sweet-smelling silk pouches.
N	Another of its aims is to remind people of the value of patriotism and loyalty to your community.
N	What's that?
N	Patriotism is being keen to look after your country and loyalty to your community means looking after those who work and live around you.
N	The most important part of the festival is celebrating the memory of Qu Yuan the emperor's court minister. He was a patriot who was honest and loyal to his people and his Emperor.
N	When did he live?
N	Qu Yuan lived during the time of the Warring States between 471 and 221 B.C. The people loved him because he was an honest, kind man. They admired him because he was clever.
N	At that time, China was broken up into several smaller kingdoms. Unfortunately they did not live in peace, fighting to try to take each other over. Qu Yuan belonged to the Zhou Empire.

(Enter the Zhou Emperor followed by Qu Yuan. Two ministers stand in the wings listening.)

Emperor	You look worried Qu Yuan. What is the problem?
Qu Yuan	Your majesty, your court is full of dishonest men. They cheat you and steal from your treasury.

(The two Ministers listening look at each other in alarm.)

Emperor	Surely not, Qu Yuan. I have always trusted people who work for me.
Qu Yuan	It's true your Majesty. You must throw out everyone who does not deal honestly with you and replace them with honest men.
Emperor	I find this hard to believe. I will think about it. Now I have to think about war against the Qin Empire.
Qu Yuan	Your Majesty, we must not go to war against them. They have a much stronger army and we would probably suffer a heavy defeat.
Emperor	If we won we would have a much greater kingdom.
Qu Yuan	If we lost we would have no kingdom at all. It would not be wise to fight

them and risk losing everything.

Emperor I will think about it, Qu Yuan.

(They exit, leaving the two court Ministers who move to centre stage.)

1st Minister Did you hear that? He has told the emperor about us.

2nd Minister I hate Qu Yuan. He is always preaching to us about right and wrong.

1st Minister We really have to get rid of him.

2nd Minister We are getting good money here. We have very comfortable lives. If the emperor finds out about all our little tricks, he'll sack us.

1st Minister It's worse than that. We could end up in prison.

2nd Minister How shall we get rid of him?

1st Minister We'll talk to the emperor and try to get him to throw Qu Yuan out.

(Enter Emperor)

Both Ministers *(Bowing)*
Good morning, Your Majesty.

Emperor Good morning, gentlemen. You look worried.

1st Minister Your Majesty, we are very worried indeed. Your Minister Qu Yuan is causing trouble in the court and the country.

Emperor Surely not. Qu Yuan is very loyal to me.

2nd Minister I'm afraid not. He turns everyone against you. The people do not care for you as they should because of his lies. He even tries to turn you against us.

Emperor I shall watch carefully. Now we must think about the war against the Qin.

1st Minister An excellent idea, your Majesty. You will be a very powerful emperor when we have beaten them.

Emperor Qu Yuan does not think so. He is against the war.

2nd Minister He does not care for your Majesty. He does not want to see you grow rich and powerful.

(The ministers move to the edge of the stage)

N Other ministers and people who worked for the emperor ganged up against Qu Yuan and eventually they persuaded the Emperor to throw him out of the Palace.

(Enter Qu Yuan)

Emperor Everywhere I go I hear tales of your disloyalty towards me. You turn my people against me. You try to stop me going to war to enlarge my empire. I don't want you in my palace ever again. Leave at once!

Qu Yuan But your Majesty, I assure you...

Emperor I'm not listening. Get out or I shall have you thrown out.

(Qu Yuan looks hurt, bows his head and walks away sadly. Ministers at the side of the stage, grin and give each other the thumbs up or high fives. They all exit.)

N   Qu Yuan went into exile. During his time abroad, he travelled and wrote books. His book 'The Lament' and the 'Nine Chapters' are masterpieces and they describe ancient Chinese culture. One day he heard some terrible news.

(Qu Yuan sitting at a table in a café. Some other Zhou people are sitting at another table.)

1st Fisherman
           We are from the Zhou Empire. Are you?

Qu Yuan   Yes, but I have not lived there for years. I am Qu Yuan. I used to be a minister for the Emperor.

1st Fisherman
           I thought you were Qu Yuan. Have you heard the news?

Qu Yuan   What news?

1st Fisherman
           The war between the Zhou and the Qin is over. The Qin have won. They now govern the Zhou Empire.

Qu Yuan   That's dreadful! This is the worst day of my life! I can't bear to hear about a foreign kingdom taking over our lovely Zhou Empire. I have always dreamed that one day I could go back to my country. Now I shall never see it again.

(Fisherman goes back to his own group of people and they mime having a drink and a chat and Qu Yuan starts writing.)

N   Qu Yuan was heart-broken. He began writing his last poem.

Qu Yuan   *(Reading as he writes)*
           Many a heavy sigh I have in my despair,
           Grieving that I was born in such an unlucky time.
           I yoked a team of jade dragons to a phoenix chariot,
           And waited for the wind to come,
           To sour up my journey.

(Exit Qu Yuan)

N   Poor Qu Yuan was so heart-broken that he went off to the Milou River and threw himself into it.

1st Fisherman
           Poor Qu Yuan! He is heart-broken about the war. I had to leave him alone. He just wanted to be by himself.

1st Woman   It was awful the way he was sent out of the kingdom. The people missed him. He always wanted to do what was best for the people.

2nd Woman   Not like the Emperor's other ministers.

(Enter waiter)

Waiter   That man who was sitting here. I can't believe what he has done. He has thrown himself into the Milou River and drowned himself.

2nd Fisherman
           That's dreadful. It's the worst news we have heard since the Qin have taken us over.

2nd Woman It is sad to think that the fish in the river will eat the body of our wonderful Qu Yuan.

1st Fisherman
    Let's go down to the river and try to pull his body out.

(They exit)

N   The legend is that people were so horrified at the idea that fish might eat Qu Yuan's body that they rushed to the river and tried to rescue it. It had disappeared and so in despair they threw food like zongzi and eggs into the river so that the fish might eat that and leave Qu Yuan's body alone.

N   Since that time, Chinese people celebrate the Dragon Boat festival by eating Zongzi. It is a special dumpling made from rice and wrapped up in bamboo leaves. Today Zongzi is made in the shape of triangles and pyramids and filled with meat, nuts, eggs, beans, dates and other fruit and vegetables.

N   Let us pray.
    Oh God help us to be honest like Qu Yuan and always show kindness and loyalty to the people around us at school and in the area where we live.

Chapter 4 Christian assemblies

St Valentine's Day

14th February

St Valentine is celebrated each year with cards and flowers and messages in newspapers, but very few people know much about St. Valentine. There are records of at least two Christian priests called Valentine during Roman times. Both were martyred. This story of Valentine appeals to people of all backgrounds because it is a story of love, courage and defiance of injustice.

> **Characters**
>
> St Valentine
> Emperor Claudius II
> 1st Roman Soldier
> 2nd Roman Soldier
> Other Roman Soldiers
> 2 girls - non-speaking parts but they can double up as narrators
> Jailer's daughter
> Lots of narrators

N	Welcome to our assembly. The 14th February is St Valentine's day. All around the globe people celebrate St Valentine's day in different ways. In Britain people send Valentine cards to their boyfriends and girlfriends to celebrate the day. In other countries people give cards to members of their family and friends.
N	But who was St Valentine?
N	There was more than one Valentine. There are records that say that in Roman times there were priests named Valentine who were put to death as Christian martyrs.
N	I prefer the story of the other Valentine, the Bishop of Terni. We can tell you all about him.
N	In the 3rd Century AD
The Romans ruled aggressively
All around the Mediterranean Sea.

(*A group of Roman soldiers line up in fours and march on the spot, looking fierce. They should be barefoot to lessen the noise.*)

N	From North Africa to the Scottish Borders,
Only the Romans gave the orders.
From Portugal to Palestine
The Roman Emperor ruled sublime.

(*Claudius II struts across the stage, looking angry.*)

N But Claudius the Second was becoming irked.
For his legionaries no longer worked
With vigour and determination
To keep up Roman domination.

(Soldiers stop marching and mime yawning and chatting to each other in groups as Claudius speaks.)

Claudius My soldiers are lazy. They don't want to fight.
I know the way to set them right.
It's love that's weakening all my men.
I'll put an end to that silly trend.

(Girls approach soldiers and begin to mime chatting with them)

N And he sent out a proclamation
To every Roman governed nation.

(As Claudius speaks the soldiers and girls turn and look at him in horror.)

Claudius No more are soldiers allowed to wed.
Too long have women turned their heads
Away from fighting to extend our empire.
I want the Romans to rise higher
Than ever in our history.
I shall be covered in triumph and glory.
Women are the cause of the army's downfall.
From now on I decree that all
My soldiers will be single men
Who will respond to orders when
I send them off to fight for me.
I'll kill any soldier who dares to marry.
Let every legionary be wary.

(Exit Claudius)

N Throughout the whole of Italy
Soldiers resented not being free
To love and marry as they chose.
They thought the new law rather gross.

N But a Christian priest named Valentine.
In disgust said

(Enter Valentine)

Valentine Men it's time
To stand up to this outrageous rule.
Forbidding love really isn't cool.
Banning marriage is absurd.

N And so he sent out the word.
If any soldier wanted a wife,
Valentine would risk his life
To perform the marriage ceremony,
In his church secretly.

N   The message spread from his town of Terni
That any soldier who would make the journey
To our hero's church, could be wed.
And lots of the soldiers went ahead.

(The rest of the class mime chatting to pass on the word and the moving on to speak to others.)

1st Roman Soldier
(Addressing crowd, holding hands with a girl or with his arm round her shoulders)

Who cares about the Roman Empire?
I've trained and fought and now I'm tired
Of battling and building roads and towns.
I've fallen in love. I want to settle down.

2nd Roman soldier   *(with girl on his arm)*
My pretty bride won't wait forever.
That wicked Claudius will never
Change his mind. This is no life.
I'll break the law and take a wife.

(Exit soldiers and girls except 2nd soldier and girl who walk towards Valentine, who beckons them into his church and mimes locking the door.)

N   And so the soldiers one by one
Went to Valentine. He told each to come
To his church with his bride.
They locked the door when they stepped inside.

(Soldier and girl kneel in front of Valentine who mimes performing service)

N   The bride and soldier were feeling nervous
As Valentine performed the service.
They thanked the priest and slipped away
To celebrate their wedding day.

(Looking pleased they shake hands with Valentine and exit. Claudius comes on at the other side of the stage looking fierce. A Roman approaches him and mimes telling him about Valentine.)

N   Claudius' anger was not soothed.
The army's success had not improved.
At last he heard about Valentine.
He was in no mood to be benign
Towards the disobedient priest.

Claudius II
Imprison him! He'll never be released.

(He exits and Valentine re-enters stage and is grabbed by two soldiers who drag him off.)

N   So our Valentine was arrested.
His faith and courage sorely tested.
He was slung into a nasty little cell.
But the people of Terni still loved him well.

(Valentine is thrown onto floor and left alone)

N They brought him food so the story goes.
And gave him strength to bear his woes.
The jailer's daughter loved our priest.
She was really rather pleased
That he had championed the lovers.
And married lots of them under-cover.

(Jailer's daughter enters with basket, sits down and chats to Valentine.)

N She brought him food and drinks and flowers.
She kept him company for hours.
Her kindness and encouragement
Made sure our priest did not relent
Or try to avoid his punishment.

(Exit jailer's daughter. Two soldiers enter and drag Valentine off-stage.)

N At last the dreadful day came along.
He lifted his head up straight and strong
When the guards came and took him away.
He was put to death that day.

(Enter jailer's daughter. Soldier mimes speaking to her.)

N The jailer's daughter was devastated
When the prison guards related
The horrid news of Valentine's death.

(She mimes crying, searching, finds a piece of 'parchment' - a piece of ragged edged paper with light brown crayoning over it. She reads it)

N She rushed to his cell and out of breath
She searched his things and found a note,
Which Valentine for her had wrote,
Thanking her for food and loving care
And all the happy hours they'd shared.
And the kindly letter was neatly signed.

Jailer's daughter *(Reading)*
With all my love, your Valentine.

N Let us pray.
Oh God help us to always be brave enough to say and do the right things and not fear other people's disapproval.

Chapter 4 Christian assemblies

St David's Day

1st March

St David, the Patron Saint of Wales, is commemorated all over Wales by the large number of churches and places named after him. The Welsh celebrate his day each year with Eisteddfods - competitions of Welsh arts and culture. Little is known about him, but he is still an important person to the Welsh.

> **Characters**
>
> St David
> Paulinus, his tutor in the monastery
> Padarn, fellow pupil
> Teilo, fellow pupil
> Monks
> Father of sick child
> Sick child
> People listening to David preaching
> Lots of narrators

Whole class Dydd gwyl Dewi hapus. (*pronounced deeth gwill daywee hapus*)

N That means 'Happy St David's day'. This week on the 1st March, Welsh people celebrate the day of St David, their Patron Saint.

N Who was St David?

N He was a Welsh monk who lived in the 6th and possibly the 5th centuries. No one knows when he was born, but he died on 1st March 589 AD. Some people say he was over 100 yeas old when he died, but no one can be certain. Let us tell you about him.

N Many centuries ago, down in the Dark Ages,
Britain had suffered many battle rages.
The Celts had come and settled here.
Great warriors they fought with sword and spear.

N The Romans, not bothered by their strength
Invaded Britain and at length,
British tribes were conquered one by one.
Some fought back but the Romans won.

N But of course no empire lasts for ever.
At last the great Romans had to sever
Their ties with Britain and go home.
Next was the turn of the Saxons to come.

N The Saxons attacked and pillaged and destroyed

	The orderly life the British enjoyed. There were many nasty, warring tales, How they drove the Britons west to Wales.
N	So into this troubled Dark Age time David was born about 489.
N	What were the Welsh like at that time?
N	They were a mixture of people descended from the ancient Bronze Age people, the Celts and the Romans who had settled here.
N	What about their religion?
N	There were some Christians because Christianity had come here during the Roman period. There were also lots of pagans and probably people with no religion.
N	What sort of family was David born into?
N	Were they rich or poor?
N	Were they Christian or pagan?
N	David's father was called Sant. His father was Ceredig, a prince of Ceridigion. David's mother was called Non and her father was a chieftain of a tribe. Some people say that she was a niece of King Arthur, but that's not proven.
N	Tell us all about his early life.
N	That's difficult. You see there was not much writing in the Dark Ages. That's why we don't know so much about them and that's why they are called the Dark Ages.
N	Nearly 500 years after his death, two people wrote about him. Rhigyfarch Gerallt Gymro tells us everything we know about him.
N	Can we be sure they got it right, if everything said about David is just handed down by word of mouth.
N	No, definitely not. Some of the stories told about David are so unlikely that we have to call them legends rather than facts.
N	David was born in South West Wales, in a town which is now called Capel Non, named after Non, his mother. His parents were Christians and sent him to a monastery to learn to read and write.

(The narrators move to the side and David and the other boys sit on the floor in front of Paulinus, their tutor, who is seated on a chair. The boys listen while Paulinus mimes talking to the group.)

N	As a boy David studied well under his blind tutor, Paulinus. He prayed regularly and wanted to spread Christianity throughout Wales.
Paulinus	Your lessons for today are now over. You have concentrated well today.

(The boys exit, leaving David, Padarn and Teilo)

David	Paulinus, I have been at Hen Fynyw (pronounced Vunyoo) Monastery since I was a child. I am happy here but I'm sure God wants me to do more with my life than just work here.
Paulinus	What do you want to do, David?
David	I want to travel round Wales. I want to spread Christianity everywhere.
Padarn	I'd love to come with you.

Teilo	So would I.
Paulinus	Then go and God will look after you on your travels. (*Exit Paulinus*)
N	So the friends got a group of men together and went off travelling round Wales. When they went to new towns and villages, they stopped to preach the gospel to the people and tell parables as Jesus had done.

(*David preaches standing in the middle of the stage and the rest of the class sit on the floor listening to him. Or you could have a few children at the side of the stage miming the story of the Good Samaritan.*)

David	Jesus told this story to show people how God wanted them to treat other people in a neighbourly way. One day, a Jewish man started walking from Jerusalem to Jericho. It was a dangerous road where travellers were often attacked and robbed. That's what happened to this poor man. A gang of thieves set upon him, beat him up horribly and stole his money leaving him to die. Along came a man who ignored him and went on his way. A few hours later, another man came along but he ignored him as well. Eventually when the poor man had given up hope, along came a Samaritan who helped him onto this donkey and took him to an inn. He paid the inn-keeper money to feed him and give him a bed and offered to come back the next day and pay any extra that the innkeeper needed for the Jewish man.
N	The people listened and David and his friends spread Christianity throughout Wales. They built lots of churches and then they went to Cornwall and Brittany. Some people say he may have gone to Ireland.

(*The class get up split into little groups to mime, hymn singing, praying, building, working in the garden.*)

N	When he had finished travelling, he set up a monastery on the site where the Cathedral of St David's stands today.
N	In his monastery, the monks got up early every day to pray and sing hymns. Then they spent the rest of their day working in the monastery gardens. They grew lots of vegetables and herbs and kept bees.
N	As far as we know, David was a vegetarian. The monks had to produce enough vegetables to feed themselves, and also to feed the poor people of the area and travellers who were passing by.
N	There are lots of stories about David. We will tell you some of them.

(*Children stop miming and exit. Distressed father rushes in.*)

Father	(*Mimes banging on the monastery door. A child can knock on seat or floor to make the sound effect.*) Open up! Open up! Hurry, my son is dying. Can someone come and pray for him?
David	I'll come. Where is your house?
Man	It's just a mile along the road, but please come quickly. (*They exit*)
N	The two men rushed off.

(*They re-enter and find the boy dead. They test his pulse, try to shake him but no response.*)

Father	He's dead. We are too late. (*He cries*)

David	It's never too late for God. (*He kneels and prays*) Oh God, please let this child stay with us. Please return him to us and let him live in his father's house.
Boy	(*Opening his eyes and sitting up*) Father.
Father	You've saved my son. You've brought him back from the dead.
David	No, my friend, God has brought him back from the dead.

(*Exit father and son. Enter Paulinus*)

N	It is impossible to tell if this story is true, but it is one of the legends of St David. Here is another one.
David	Paulinus, how long have you been blind?
Paulinus	Many years, David, but I have tried not to let it stop me doing God's work.
David	Wouldn't you like to see again, Paulinus?
Paulinus	Of course I would.
David	(*Praying*) Oh God please give Paulinus back his eyesight, so that he can enjoy the beauty of your world and be better able to do your work.
Paulinus	(*Rubs his eyes and looks around and then at David*) I can see, David. God has cured my blindness.
N	The most famous and most amazing story about David took place at the Synod of Llanddewi Brefi. A Synod is a meeting of important church leaders who discuss church matters and make decisions. This Synod wanted to choose a new Archbishop for Wales.
N	A huge crowd of people met to hear David.

(*David is at the back of the stage standing in front of a chair. He is obscured by most of the rest of the class who are standing with their backs to the rest of the school.*)

Person from the crowd
  We can't see you, David.

N	Miraculously the ground underneath David rose so everyone could see and hear him.

(*David steps backward onto the chair and slowly raises his head and shoulders above the crowd.*)

N	There are no prizes for guessing who was selected as Archbishop of Wales after that.

(*The class turn round to face the audience again.*)

N	Why do the Welsh have a leek as an emblem?
N	Long ago the Welsh fought against Saxons who had taken over England. Armies did not wear uniforms in those days so David suggested that the Welsh put a leek into their helmets so that they could tell the Welshmen from the Saxons.
N	The daffodil was introduced as an emblem much later.

N	Today, in Wales, every year on 1st March children go to school but instead of having lessons they have competitions of Welsh songs, dances, poetry, and art. This celebration is called an Eisteddfod. The children pin a leek or a daffodil to their jumpers.
N	In some Welsh schools the children wear Welsh national costume. The girls wear a tall beaver hat with a white frill around the base, a white blouse with a red shawl and black skirt. The boys wear a white shirt with frills round the wrist, a Welsh flannel waist coat, black knee-length breeches with long socks.
N	Welsh people love to sing hymns and it is a national tradition. We are going to finish with a hymn.

Whole class sings any hymn which they learnt recently.

N	Let us pray. Oh God, thank you for the life of St David. Whatever our race or religion, help us to keep our faith in it and to be able to have pleasure in enjoying our own and other people's culture.

Chapter 4   Christian assemblies

St Patrick's Day

17th March

In Ireland, many schools close for a whole or a half day for their Patron Saint's day. His day is celebrated with great enthusiasm in New York where there is a large Irish population. Like St David, there is little information about St Patrick available. Most of it is handed down by word of mouth. The serious traditional story of St Patrick and the humorous fairy story make a balanced performance.
This script works well if the action is slick.

St Patrick

> **Characters**
>
> Patrick
> King Laoghaire (pronounced Leery)
> Raiders
> Captives
> Monks
> King's men
> Lots of narrators

The Leprechaun's Gold

> **Characters**
>
> Sean the leprechaun (the smallest child in the class)
> The farmer, Darby O' Toole (the tallest)
> Narrators

N	Good morning everyone and welcome to our assembly. This week on 17th March, Irish people are celebrating the feast day of their Patron Saint, St Patrick.

N	Our class are going to tell you the story of St Patrick in rhyme and mime.

N	St Patrick was born long ago
	In England or Wales. We really don't know.

N	Sometime round about 389.
	A sturdy lad in Roman times,

(*Patrick strides across the stage, flexing his muscles and looking sturdy.*)

N	Patrick grew up in a Christian family,
	Studied Latin and lived quite happily.

(Patrick mimes reading, while his mother and father look on, pat his back and move away.)

N	Until one day Patrick was snatched
	By Irish raiders and dispatched
	In a slave boat off to the Emerald Isle.

(Two or three raiders stride across the stage, grab Patrick, one under each arm and drag him off to the edge of the stage.)

N	Terrified, he waited while
	His parents sought him anxiously.
	Patrick crossed the Irish Sea.

(At one side of the stage, Patrick sits in the middle of a group of captives, crying and looking terrified. Parents on the other side are searching anxiously and then they move away.)

N	In Ireland frightened and distraught
	By a farmer, Milchu, he was bought
	And sent out onto the bleak Mount Slemish
	To mind the pigs and sheep, and famish
	Among the animals with nought to eat
	But cold leftovers of animal feed.

(Slave-trader leads the unhappy Patrick, head bowed and hands behind his back as if bound and hands him over for money to Milchu who leads him across the stage to where several children are on all fours as pigs and sheep.)

N	His Christian background gave him strength
	To go on living; and at length,
	One night he escaped and took a chance
	And stowed away on a boat to France.

(Patrick sneaks away and starts walking a short way from the stage and back to it.)

N	He journeyed south towards the tideless sea
	And joined a Christian monastery.

N	He prayed and preached and read books in Latin.
	He sang at Evensong and Matins.

(Patrick mimes praying, reading or singing alongside other monks.)

N	Then one night in a harrowing dream
	He heard the Irish calling him.

(Patrick lies down and sleeps,)

The rest of the class as Irish people
	'Come back to Ireland we need you here!'

N	Patrick, startled, began to fear.
	Dare he go back to that dreadful place?

(Patrick wakes up terrified)

N *(Aside)*	The Irish were such a heathen race!

Patrick	Am I meant to be God's missionary To bring to them Christianity?	
N	Undaunted, Patrick packed his case And journeyed back to the dreaded place.	

(*Patrick mimes journeying, coming off the boat.*)

N	Patrick arrived there, tired and weary, Just as the Great High King Laoghaire Was about to start a Pagan feast By lighting his beacon in the east.	(pronounced Leery)

(*Patrick arrives, yawning and looking weary and then he lights a beacon.*)

N Undaunted, Patrick lit one first.
That really was about the worst
Crime that he could have committed.
Laoghaire would not be outwitted.

King Laoghaire (*Angrily pointing at Patrick*)
Bring me that man! At the double!
He is in a lot of trouble.

(*Laoghaire's men grab Patrick and bring him to the king.*)

N This is what our Patrick planned
To meet King Laoghaire man to man.

(*Patrick bows respectfully to the king and then mimes talking to him.*)

N He seized the opportunity
To convert the king and his community.

N He told him of the birth of Jesus Christ
And how at Easter he was sacrificed.

N To explain the Trinity he looked around
And saw some shamrocks on the ground.

(*Patrick looks at the floor and picks a large green shamrock made of sugar paper off the ground.*)

N He showed how each leaf was in three
To demonstrate the Trinity.
(*Points to the three heart-shaped leaves*)

N Ireland became a Christian land.
They built great churches and cathedrals grand.

N And Patrick spent the rest of his days
Teaching the Irish, Christian ways.

N And when his lifetime was all spent.
They made our hero their patron saint.

N Today the Irish have the shamrock as their national emblem in memory of St Patrick using it to explain the trinity to the king.

N Telling fairy stories is a very old tradition in Ireland. Our form are going to entertain

	you with a popular Irish tale.
	Or
N	Our class are now going to treat you all to a wee bit of high class Irish culture. *(Give this line to the child who can best mimic an Irish accent.)*
N	**THE LEPRECHAUN'S GOLD** *(Sean mimes all of this while the narrators tell the story.)*
N	Early one bright, spring morning, Sean the Leprechaun stepped out of his home inside the hollowed out oak tree. He stretched himself in the sun and took a deep breath of fresh air.
N	He stamped his feet on the soft earth round the oak tree and rubbed his sleeves and trousers to knock the tiny pieces of wood and leaf off his clothes.
N	Then he reached back into his home to pull out his rucksack. Looking carefully inside, he checked that his gold was still there.
N	He heaved the rucksack onto his back and began weaving his way, in and out around the trees until he came to the frogs' pond. He tiptoed round it, so he would not disturb any of the woodland creatures who were still fast asleep.
N	When he passed the owl's nest, high up in an old elm tree, he was very careful indeed, because he knew that she had been up all night hunting, and would not want to be wakened by the clinking of Sean's gold coins.
N	He almost went too near the drey, where Bushy the squirrel was sleeping, but he did not dare, because once already, Bushy had pushed her curious head into his rucksack and tried to steal one of his coins.
N	She was becoming rather blind, in her old age, and was not always sure what she was biting.
N	At last he came to the edge of the wood and found himself in an enormous field covered with gorse bushes.

(You can have a screen with a field of gorse bushes reflected off an overhead projector or PowerPoint.)

Sean	Here's a good place to hide my gold. No one will find it if I bury it beneath a gorse bush.
N	*(Sean still miming)* He dropped his rucksack onto the ground and opened it. He lifted out a little spade and began to shovel the earth away near the roots of one of the bushes.
N	Soon the hole was so deep that when he stood in it, he could not see over the top without standing on the tips of his toes, so he climbed out and lifted his precious bag of gold out of his rucksack. He made certain that it was tied tightly at the top, and gently lowered it into the hole.

(Sean kneels and mimes looking over the top of a hole.)

N	He covered it with earth and took a ball of yellow ribbons out of the pocket of his baggy trousers. He tied one of his ribbons tightly round the gorse bush. *(If you have a large potted plant in the school you can put in onto the stage for Sean to tie on his ribbon. Otherwise just mime.)*

N	Content with his work, he replaced the spade in his rucksack and the ribbons in his pocket and began making his way home for breakfast.
N	He hopped and skipped happily round the gorse bushes until he reached the river again, but just as he was about to leap over the water, two large hands grasped poor Sean so tightly, he was petrified...

(*Sean hops and skips and the farmer, Darby O'Toole, steps out from the side and grabs him.*)

Darby O'Toole	(*Aggressively, with a nasty grin*) Where have you hidden your gold?
Sean	(*Stammering, terrified, but trying to sound brave*) I'm not telling you.
Darby	Where have you hidden your gold?
N	He shook Sean by the shoulders so hard that his rucksack fell off his shoulders and tumbled into the river.
Darby	'TELL ME WHERE YOUR GOLD IS, OR I SHALL THROW YOU INTO THE RIVER AS WELL AS YOUR RUCKSACK!'
N	Sean could not swim, and he was so terrified that he stammered that his gold was under the gorse bush with the yellow ribbon tied to it.
Darby	Good! I'm going home for my spade. You'll never see your gold again!

(*Darby storms off the stage.*)

N	Poor Sean was heart-broken. (*Sean crying*) He had lost his spade in the river and could not dig his gold up in time to stop Darby having it. He had tied the knot on the yellow ribbon so tightly that he could not possibly untie it. Then he had a terrific idea.

(*Sean grins mischievously.*)

N	He dried his eyes, rubbed his aching shoulders and lifted the ball of yellow ribbons out of his pocket.

(*Overlay the gorse bushes on the screen with another ohp sheet putting dozens of yellow ribbons onto the gorse bushes or have a second slide on the Power Point display.*)

N	An hour later when Darby O' Toole returned to the field, every single gorse bush had a yellow ribbon tied to it.

(*Darby enters, looks horrified and angry*)

N	Furious that he had been tricked by the clever leprechaun, Darby stormed off home in disgust.

(*Darby storms off in disgust*)

N	Sean came out of his hiding place behind the horse chestnut tree and laughed merrily as he skipped off home to find his other spade.

(*Sean giggles and skips off*)

(*Children love to sing. There are lots of books around with Irish songs which you can teach them. You may be lucky and have an Irish child in the class who can perform an Irish jig.*)

N Let us pray.
Oh God, help us to be brave like St Patrick when things go wrong for us. Help us to remember that You will always help us to cope with every difficulty.

Christian

Chapter 4 Christian assemblies

Easter

March/April

Easter is the most important festival of the Christian calendar, although Christmas may be more popular.

This script could become complicated if one tried to use furniture and props. It works better if they are all omitted. The number of actions might be too many for Lower Juniors so some actions could be cut and have some verses just narrated.

> **Characters**
>
> Jesus
> Peter
> John
> James
> Judas
> Thomas
> Other disciples
> Mary, Jesus' mother
> Mary Magdalene
> Pilate
> Two robbers on crosses
> Joseph of Arimathea
> High Priest
> Priests
> Two men on the way to Emmaus
> The priests' men
> People listening to Jesus
> Narrators (Any of the above, except Jesus, can double up as narrators.)

(Jesus in the middle of the stage, miming giving a sermon, most of the rest of the class, seated on the floor, listening to him.)

N   In the year AD34
                Around the Med's eastern shore,
                Jesus had spent three years teaching,
                Praying, healing and gospel preaching.

N   When Jesus entered a village or town,
                Lots of people gathered round.
                They loved to hear his sermons and parables.
                His calm, serene voice turned all the rabbles
                Into listeners eager to learn.

(Two or three priests enter at the side of the stage, whispering and looking annoyed as they watch. Jesus and the crowd gradually disperse to the sides of the stage, being careful not to mask the priests.)

N	But some of the priests started to yearn For the days when everyone listened to them. They felt threatened each time when They saw that the people much preferred Jesus' advice to what they heard In the temple from their priests, And their influence was being decreased.

(Jesus moves centre stage with some disciples and the class, as the crowd comes to greet him, putting down palm leaves of green sugar paper. Priests still watching and becoming angry.)

N	The disciples and Jesus came to Jerusalem And the crowd gathered to welcome them. On a donkey Jesus met the crowd Who thronged the streets and shouted aloud,
People	Hosanna Jesus, Hosanna to the King. Let the streets with pleasure ring.
N	They laid their garments on the ground And put fresh palm leaves all around For Jesus to ride in majesty. The priests now were seriously Troubled by his popularity.

(Crowd disperses to the edge of the stage. Some remain to be money changers. Jesus strides into the temple.)

N	Into the temple Jesus went. The money-changers were horribly bent. They were charging dreadful prices. Jesus thought it the worst of vices For people needed money to buy sacrifices.

(Jesus looks angry, wags his finger, mimes speaking angrily and overturning tables. He points to the door to order money-changers out. Priests look outraged.)

N	This dishonest practice he angrily spurned. Their tables of money he overturned. This angered all the priests And their patience completely ceased.

(Everyone exits, except priests)

N	Love for Jesus grew and grew. The high priests worked out what to do And secretly they began to plan.
High Priest	We have got to get rid of this man! We need a traitor. Who will betray him? Who will help us if we pay him?

(Enter Judas)

N   Along came the disciple Judas.
They showed him thirty silver pieces.

(They mime showing Judas the money and he looks pleased.)

High Priest   These are yours if you will please us
By leading us to this man Jesus.

N   A poor man, Judas, he acted rash.
Stretched out his hand and took the cash.

(Judas takes money and exits. Priests look at each other contentedly and exit on the other side of the stage. Jesus enters with disciples and they sit down on the floor for their Passover meal.)

N   Now at this time Jews celebrated
Their ancestors being liberated
From slavery in Egypt centuries ago.
They gathered together each year to show
Their thanks for saving them from their foe.

N   'Passover' is the name of the event.
To an upper room the disciples went.
Jesus took a loaf and broke the bread.

(Jesus mimes breaking bread and pouring wine and they pass it round.)

Jesus   This is my body. Eat it,

N   he said.
He lifted the wine and spoke solemnly,

Jesus   My blood. Drink it and remember me.

N *(Aside)*   In memory of Jesus, Christians today
Have wine and bread on Communion day.

N   He looked at his friends and said

Jesus   This is the last
Time we'll share a happy repast.
Tomorrow I shall be arrested.
Pray for me. My strength will be tested.
In a hostile court I shall be tried
And then I shall be crucified.

N   His disciples all were horrified.

John   How can this be? You have done no wrong.

Jesus   The High Priest wants to slay me.
One of you will betray me!

Peter   No one here could do you wrong.
I shall stand by you my whole life long.

Jesus   Sadly, Peter, that will not be
When the cock crows you'll have denied me
Three times. Now I need to rest and pray.
To prepare for tomorrow, my trial day.

(*They exit and re-enter in the garden.*)

N They entered the Garden of Gethsemane.
Jesus went to pray quietly.

Jesus Peter, James and John, guard the gate.

(*They wait by the gate and fall asleep.*)

N Now Jesus, human, thought of his fate.

Jesus (*Praying*)
Father even at this late
Hour I beg you, if you can
Save me. I'm only a man.

N But Jesus got his strength from prayer.
Suddenly the High Priest's men were there.

(*High Priest's men enter with Judas who goes up to Jesus and kisses him.*)

N Judas went to Jesus and kissed him
They arrested Jesus. He did not resist them.

(*Peter awakens and lunges his sword towards a priest's man who howls and holds the side of his head, because Peter has chopped off his ear.*)

Jesus (*to Peter*) You shouldn't have done that! (*To the man*) Do not fear.

(*Jesus replaces the ear.*)

N Jesus lifted the ear and healed the man.
The disciples were scared and away they ran.

(*The disciples run away. The High Priest and other priests enter.*)

N Next day the Jewish Council tried Jesus.

High priest Your behaviour much displeases!
Are you the Messiah, the son of God?

Jesus I am. (*Jesus nods*)

N He answered with a nod.

High Priest Enough of this dreadful blasphemy!
You are a man of detestable infamy!
You will go to the Governor, Pilate.
And his sentence will seal your fate.

(*Jesus is taken away and they all exit. The crowd of people, including the disciples, enter. The priests move around the crowds talking to them.*)

N Now at that time it was the tradition
To choose a prisoner and give him permission
To leave the jail and go back home.

N And some hoped Jesus would be the one.

	But the priests had already begun Stirring up the crowd to shout To let Barabbas, another prisoner, out.

(Peter and a woman move to the front, centre stage.)

N	Meanwhile in the crowd a woman Saw a frightened man roaming On his own, avoiding company.
Woman	You and Jesus were very friendly.
Peter	No!
Woman	Yes you were. I saw you by him.
Peter	No!
Woman	Yes. Why do you deny him?
Peter	No!
N	Peter's promise had not been kept. *(Sound of cock crowing)* A rooster crowed and Peter wept.

(The people move to one side of the stage.)

N	Next day Jesus faced the Governor. He suffered mockery and torture.

(Enter Pilate, High Priest and other priests. Jesus is brought in.)

Pilate	Do you call yourself the Jewish king?
N	But Jesus would not say anything.
N	Pilate could see that the priests were jealous. He wanted order, not long and zealous Arguments and people in riot. He'd like to free Jesus but dared not try it.
Pilate	What shall I do with Jesus of Nazareth?
People	Crucify!
N	was on their breath. Pilate gave in to the demands of them. Had Jesus condemned and washed his hands of him.

(Exit Pilate. The crowd gets into two groups with an aisle up the centre for Jesus to trail up his cross.)

N	Jesus trailed his cross out of the city. Some cheered with delight and some wept in pity. Three stark crosses on Golgotha stood. Two robbers and Jesus were nailed to the wood.

(Jesus and two others stand up with arms out stretched, Jesus in the middle. The crowd stands back, except Mary and John nearby.)

Robber 1   Save yourself, and both of us too.

Robber 2   This is our own fault. We knew
That we were men of sin and vice.

Jesus (*To 2nd robber*)
To-day you will be with me in Paradise.

N   Jesus looked down at the base of his cross.
John and his mother were at a loss
To know what to do or what to say.

Jesus   Mother, John will be your son from this day.
And John, love Mary in a son-like way.

N   And sadly Jesus died.
Mary, his mother, cried.

(*Exit Mary and John. Enter Joseph of Arimathea and Pilate.*)

N   Joseph of Arimathea went to Pilate.

Joseph of Arimathea
Our Lord is dead. Will you permit
Me to take his body down
To bury it properly in the ground.
I have, in my garden, hewn
Into the rock to make a tomb.

N   Pilate didn't really care.

Pilate   You can take it anywhere.

(*Enter Mary, Mary Magdalene, John and Peter. They go to Jesus and lift him and carry him off stage. This can be done if each boy takes a shoulder and an arm and each girl takes a leg.*)

N   So the body was lifted carefully
And laid in the tomb tenderly.
Mary and Mary Magdalene, his most loved women
Wept as they wrapped him in purest linen.

N   Joseph covered the tomb with an enormous stone.

(*Joseph mimes rolling stone across the tomb and exits.*)

N   Next day was the Sabbath so they stayed at home.
But on Sunday they had to come.

(*They re-enter, Jesus behind them*)

N   Back to the garden to move the stone
Away from the tomb and go inside.
But when they got there they were horrified.

N   The stone was moved. Jesus wasn't there.
They searched but couldn't find him anywhere.
Anxiously they turned and saw a man.

(*Mary Magdalene turns and sees Jesus.*)

Mary Magdalene
Please tell me if you can,
Where is Jesus? Have you taken him away?

Jesus Mary. I have risen from the dead.
I am going to my Father in Heaven,

N He said.

Jesus Go and tell everyone you know.
I've risen from the dead and I shall show
Everyone my resurrection.
My disciples must go out in all directions
And tell the world of my words and affections.
Spread the Gospel into every land
Teach every child and woman and man
Of their place in Heaven by God's right hand.

(*Exit everyone except Jesus. Enter two men walking to Emmaus.*)

N Jesus appeared a few times more.
To men on the road walking to Emmaus
Leaving Jerusalem to escape from the chaos.

(*The men look stunned and turn and rush back to Jerusalem.*)

People saw him walking by the lake.
They rushed to the city to take
The news that Jesus had risen from the dead.

(*The men re-enter with the disciples.*)

Thomas I won't believe it until I see it,

N Thomas said.

Jesus From now on all the doubt and fear ends.
All of you go and tell the world I am alive.
Make sure all my teachings survive.
Go to every country round the sea.
Make sure everyone knows about Me.

N And so the disciples became missionaries.
They journeyed over lands and seas.
They preached the Gospel on the way,
So Christianity survives today.

N Let us pray.
Jesus, thank you for the wonderful sacrifice you made on the cross. Help us to keep your laws and always be willing to be kind to others, to please you.

Chapter 4 Christian assemblies

St George's Day

23rd April

Although St George is the Patron Saint of England, almost nothing is known about the real man. He is perhaps best known as the man who slew the dragon to save the maiden.

> **Characters**
>
> Villagers
> The village chief
> The chief's daughter
> St George
> The dragon
> Lots of narrators

N — Good morning and welcome to our assembly. This week on April 23rd it will be the feast day of St George, the patron saint of England.

N — What do we know about him?

N — Actually, very little. There is more fiction than fact known about St George. We think that he lived in Asia Minor in the 3rd century AD. He was a Christian and he was put to death for his faith. The word for someone who is killed for their beliefs is 'martyr', so he is sometimes known as 'St George the Martyr'.

N — Some accounts say that he was put to death and he came to life to be martyred again and again, but of course that's not proven.

N — He was made the Patron Saint of England by Edward III. His flag was a red addition cross on a white banner and was first adopted by Richard I, who is known as Richard the Lionheart.

N — Richard I was a warlike king. He went off to the continent to fight the Wars of the Crusades. The story is that one day during a battle, the English army was flagging and they were losing heart. A vision of St George rose up before them and encouraged them to keep fighting and so they rallied their forces and eventually won the battle. King Richard adopted St George's flag as the flag of England.

N — St George is probably best known for saving the maiden from the dragon. There are lots of versions of the story and of course they must be seen as a piece of folklore, not taken seriously. We will tell you the story.

(A busy scene, children playing, mothers walking to the pond with buckets and filling them with water.)

N — Long ago in a far off land
A wooden fence round a village stands
To protect its people from robbing pillagers.

	And every day the women villagers Walked down the hill to the pond to take Some water home to drink and bake.
N	One day as the children skipped to the water, They were shocked to spy a fearful marauder.

(*Dragon arises and roars. Mothers and children look terrified.*)

	A dragon rose from the depths of the pool With dazzling red eyes, angry and full Of hunger and thirst for a tasty meal.
N	Its fiery howling made the villagers reel. With horror they froze, petrified. The children squealed and the babies cried. The mothers dropped their buckets and pans, Grabbed their children and speedily ran Back to the village and slammed the gate.

(*Mothers grab children and run. Dragon follows.*)

N	And there with bated breath they waited 'Til the dragon lurched to the gate and berated The anguished people with threats that he Would burn their village mercilessly Unless each day, they supplied A live creature to keep him satisfied.
N	They trembled in horror and shook in their shoes, And argued and fought, deciding whose Goats and sheep would be surrendered To keep their lovely town defended From this ghastly monster from the depths of the earth.
1st Villager	Should we fight him? Is it worth Risking our lives to save our homes?
2nd Villager	Should we just feed him when he comes?'
3rd Villager	A pig today, tomorrow a sheep.
4th Villager	If we do, that would keep This dreadful, murdering monster at bay.
N	So at once it was decided The savage dragon would be provided With a meal each day 'til it devoured Every animal. Then it glowered.
Dragon	Bring me a human, one each day. My appetite hasn't gone away.
N	The people wrote their names on stone

(*Mime writing, putting stones into pot and drawing lots.*)

And into a pot each was thrown.
And every day they picked out a name
Of the one to tremble 'til the dragon came.

N	One day the chief's beautiful daughter Was picked to be taken to the slaughter. The chief fainted in disbelief. (*He faints.*) The villagers ignored his grief.
5th Villager	If it wasn't his child, it would be one of us.
N	Immediately without a fuss, They pushed the maiden through the gate And tied her up to await her fate.

(*Two people mime dragging the frightened girl to the gate and tying her up.*)

N	O'er the hill came a knight on a pure white horse. It was our brave St George, of course.

(*St George enters and approaches girl.*)

George	Why are you crying, my pretty maid?
Maid	The dragon will eat me. I'm so afraid.
N	Jumping off his trusty steed, He had the maiden quickly freed. (*He frees the girl.*)
George	Where is this dragon? Where is my sword?
N	The dragon rose from the lake and roared. Lashing its head and breathing fire, It climbed the hill, higher and higher. 'Til it reached our hero on horseback.

(*Dragon arises and approaches St George and they mime the fight.*)

N	Then it swiftly lunged into attack. The dragon howled and roared and gnashed. With smoke and fire it thundered and lashed.

(*The villagers gather round*)

N	The villagers who had heard the rumpus Had left their village to encompass The fighting pair, to cheer our knight As the battle raged on day and night.

(*Dragon falls and George stabs it*)

N	'Til the dragon slumped onto his side George stabbed it and it slowly died.

(*People cheer*)

N	With joy the people celebrated. A massive feast was soon created. They sang and danced and laughed and gorged And drank a toast to the brave St George.

N   Let us pray.
Oh God, help us always to be willing to help people who are in difficulty. Make us proud of our country as well as respectful towards people of other countries.

Chapter 4 Christian assemblies

St Francis' Day

4th October

St Francis is one of the lesser known Christian saints. His story is popular with children who like animals. He is the Patron Saint of nature and the environment.

> **Characters**
>
> St Francis
> Pietro, his father
> Pica, his mother
> 3 Friends
> 2 Perugian soldiers
> A voice
> A beggar
> Monks
> Villagers
> A wolf
> Lots of narrators

N Good morning and welcome to our assembly. This week on 4th October it will be St Francis' day. We would like to tell you about him.

N Our story begins in Italy in the prosperous town of Assisi. In the late 12th century, there lived a wealthy cloth merchant and his family. His name was Pietro di Bernardone and his wife's name was Pica.

N They had several children, one of whom was born in 1181 or 1182 and named Francesco, which is the Italian for Francis. Pietro and Pica were devoted to their children and had plenty of money to make sure they were all well educated.

N First they went to a school named St George's and were taught by priests and then they attended the school of the Troubadours. Francis loved learning languages and was able to speak several including Latin.

N He spent his youth living it up, wearing fine clothes, spending lots of money having fun and going to parties and drinking with his friends. Actually he was rather spoilt.

N Even so, even as a spoilt teenager, he showed some kindness towards the poor.

(Enter a beggar in ragged clothes. He sits by the side of the stage, begging. Francis and three friends, enter at the opposite side, well dressed, laughing and enjoying themselves on the way back from a party.)

1st friend That was a great party! Giovanni still knows how to pour the wine.

Beggar	Can you spare a few coins for a poor man?
2nd Friend	He knows where to find lots of pretty girls.
Beggar	(*A little louder*) Can you spare a few coins for a poor man?
3rd Friend	When is our next party, chaps?
Beggar	(*Louder still*) Can you spare a few coins for a poor man?
1st Friend	Lucio is having a party on Saturday for his birthday.
Beggar	(*Shouting*) Can you spare a few coins for a poor man?
Francis	Yes. I have some money to spare.
2nd Friend	You must be mad. Why are you bothering with him?
Francis	(*Emptying his purse*) Here you are sir. Go and buy yourself a meal in a café.

(*The beggar exits.*)

3rd Friend	He's a beggar. We don't need to give them any money.
Francis	Yes, we should. He's hungry. We can afford to give him a little for food.

(*Enter Pietro and Pica.*)

Pica	(*Laughing*) Hello lads. Had a good night out?
Francis	Yes, dad, terrific party.
1st Friend	You'll never guess what silly old Francis has done. He's emptied his purse for a beggar.
Pietro	You fool! Why did you do that?
Francis	Because I felt sorry for him, Father.
Pietro	I have to work hard for my money. I don't give it to you to waste on beggars.
Francis	But the poor man was starving Father.
Pica	But it's his own fault if he is poor. Don't you ever throw our money away on the poor again!

(*They all exit*)

N	Francis finished off his education and joined his father in the cloth business.

(*Enter Francis and Pietro*)

Pietro	Here, Francis. This is a list of cloths to be packed up for our next trip to France. Can you have them ready in about two hours?
Francis	(*Unenthusiastically*) Yes, Father.
Pietro	And after that there's the order for the Rossi family.
Francis	Yes Father.
Pietro	Why are you so miserable? You are lucky to have a good job with good pay. You are so good at enjoying yourself but you don't want to work for the money to pay for it!

Francis	Yes Father. I would rather do something exciting than stand here all day sorting out bales of cloth.
Pietro	You are ungrateful. I have worked at it for many years to give you a comfortable life and an education.

(*Exit Pietro and Francis*)

N	Francis was not interested in the cloth trade. In 1201 when he was about twenty years old, he joined the army and went off to fight against Perugia.

(*Enter Francis and two Perugian soldiers. They mime fighting for a few seconds. Then the soldiers grab Francis, taking one arm each and drag him off stage.*)

N	Francis was thrown into prison for a whole year.

(*Francis re-enters and sits down looking sad and prays.*)

N	During this period he thought a lot about his life and realised that he was not happy. He had not been satisfied with life while he was wasting his time going to parties. He was never satisfied as a cloth merchant and he certainly didn't like sitting in prison, bored all day. He prayed to God to show him how to live a worthwhile life.

(*Exit Francis*)

N	He was allowed out of prison a year later and he returned to Assisi. He decided to join the army again and began making his way towards Spoleto to join the army. On the way there he had a dream one night.

(*Enter Francis. He lies down to sleep.*)

N	A voice said to him.
Voice	Go back to Assisi!

(*Francis awoke and returned to Assisi believing that this was what God wanted him to do.*)

N	When he returned, he often ran into his old friends.
2nd Friend	Hi Francis, we haven't seen you for weeks, come and join us at Giovanni's house tomorrow night. He has invited a few girls round. We'll have a great laugh.
Francis	I don't think so.
3rd Friend	What's wrong with you Francis? You've forgotten how to enjoy yourself.
1st Friend	Are you thinking of getting married?

(*The three friends laugh*)

Francis	Yes, I'm thinking of marrying the Lady Poverty.
2nd Friend	Are you mad?
3rd friend	Come on Francis, come to the party.
Francis	I'm not in the mood. You go. Have a good time.

(*The friends exit. Enter a leper who sits by the side of the stage begging.*)

N	One day Francis was out walking and he noticed a leper by the side of the road. The leper was so ugly with the disease that at first Francis looked away. Then he felt sorry for the man and returned, hugged him and gave him some money.

(Francis walks past him and returns to give him a hug and some money.)

N	Francis also went on a pilgrimage to Rome. He was so sad when he saw the poverty there. He gave lots of money and clothes to some poor people. He returned to Assisi and one day he was praying in front of a crucifix in the broken down chapel of St Damien when he heard a voice.
Voice	Go, Francis and repair my house which is falling into ruin.
N	Francis thought this meant that God wanted him to repair the broken down church of St Damien so he went off to his father's shop and took a load of coloured cloth. Then he sold his horse and took the money and cloth to the Church and gave it to the priest for the church. Pietro and Pica were furious.
Pica	You took all that cloth without our permission.
Francis	But it was for a church Mother. God told me to repair it.
Pietro	And that lovely horse, I bought you. You sold it and gave the money away. You are a complete fool! Get out of my house before I beat you and throw you out.
N	Francis left and his father decided to disown him forever.
Pietro	I will give you no more money and I will not leave you anything in my will. You are no longer my son.
Francis	That's fine with me. I will go and join a monastery.
N	Francis eventually started up a monastic order of his own. They were called the Franciscan Order. They took a vow of poverty and spent the rest of their lives in worship and prayer and preaching the Gospel.
N	One of their first tasks was to complete the repairs to the church of St Damien. The Franciscan monks then went on to other churches.
N	There are so many stories about Francis and animals and birds. On one occasion, Francis stood up to preach to a huge crowd of people. There were masses of birds on the trees around them so he could not be heard.

(The rest of the class make bird tweeting noises as Francis stands up to talk to them.)

Francis	(*Calling to the birds above their singing*) My friends, I cannot talk to these people because of your birdsong. Please be silent so that the people can hear me.

(The birds are silent at once.)

N	So Francis was able to preach his sermon. We would like to tell you the story of St Francis and the Wolf. One day, Francis and his companions entered a village to find the people very unhappy.

(Enter villagers to meet Francis and other monks.)

Francis	What's wrong? Why does everyone look so anxious?
1st Villager	There is a wolf prowling around the hills. He comes into our village at all hours of

	the day looking for food. He not only eats our animals, he attacks people to eat them as well.
2nd Villager	We are terrified to go out.
Francis	Where can I find him?
3rd Villager	His den is up in those hills.
Francis	I'll go and see him.
4th Villager	Be careful. Take a pitchfork with you. He is likely to attack you and kill you.
Francis	No he won't. God will protect me.

(Exit the villagers. Francis starts walking until he meets the wolf.)

Francis (*Holding out his hand in welcome*) My friend, I have come to talk to you. The villagers are unhappy because you eat their animals and even the people in the village. I know you have to eat like everyone else, but it is making everyone unhappy if you kill people. If I talk to the people and ask them to leave food for you at the entrance of the village will you promise to stop attacking them?

(Wolf nods his head and Francis leads him back to the village where the people look amazed as they enter. Villagers gather round warily.)

Francis My friends, I have talked to our friend the wolf. He has agreed to stop coming into the village and attacking people as long as you all agree to leave a day's food for him at the entrance of the village every morning. Will you all agree to do that for him so that you can all live in peace?

Villagers (*Nodding*) Yes, that's fine. Yes, we agree. Yes, we'll do that.

N And so the villagers and the wolf lived peacefully. Francis is known for his love of all living creatures. There is a legend that once he was walking along a road with his monks and there were hundreds of birds around them in the air and on the ground and on the trees. Francis, who always looked on animals and birds as fellow creatures was so delighted by the appearance of them that he stopped to preach to them, quoting from Jesus' Sermon on the Mount.

Francis You birds are my brothers and sisters. God has done so much for you that you must always praise Him. He allows you to fly freely through the air and although you do not weave or spin God has clothed you. You do not reap or sow but God feeds you. He has given you mountains and valleys and trees to nest in. So always praise God for His gifts to you.

N St Francis and his monks spent the rest of their lives travelling to countries on the Mediterranean Sea, preaching the gospel. Francis died on 4th October 1226 and was made a saint two years later in 1228. He is the patron saint of nature and the environment.

N Let us pray.
Dear God, help us to be kind to all living things. Whether they are animals or birds or people who are ill, help us to remember they we are all your children.

Chapter 4 Christian assemblies

St Andrew's Day

30th November

St Andrew, who was a fisherman of Gallilee at the time of Jesus Christ, later became one of Jesus' disciples. Some people believe that after Jesus' death, he travelled as far as Russia in spreading the gospel. He is the Patron Saint of Scotland and Russia.

> **Characters**
>
> St Andrew
> Simon Peter
> Jesus Christ
> James
> John
> A few other fishermen
> Other disciples
> A crowd of people
> Narrators who double up with disciples and members of the crowd

N Welcome to our assembly. On 30th November it will be St Andrew's day. St Andrew is the Patron Saint of Scotland and Russia. We would like to tell you about St Andrew.

(Andrew and Simon Peter with others by the side of the stage mime getting into their boat, putting their nets into the water and guiding their sail.)

N Two thousand years ago in Roman times
   Rome governed the Jews in Palestine.

N Jordan River flowed through the sand
   Giving life to the desert land.

N 'Til it reached the tiny inland sea
   By the sunny banks of Galilee.

N Fishermen went to sea each night
   As the sun was sinking out of sight.

N They put their boats on the calm, dark sea
   And lowered their nets quietly
   Into the water teeming with food.

N Andrew and Peter his brother stood
   On the deck waiting for the nets to pull
   On the edge of the boat, when they were full.

(Andrew and Peter stand at the front watching their nets.)

N	Andrew and the men waited patiently 'Til morning, and sailed to the edge of the sea.

(They start dragging the nets into the boat.)

N	They dragged their nets onto the beach, Where Jesus Christ had come to teach.

(Jesus enters)

Jesus	'Leave your nets and follow me, then I will make you fishers of men.'
N	They left their catch instantly And followed Jesus obediently.
N	They strolled together by Galilee And met James and John, sons of Zebedee.

(Enter John and James)

Jesus	Leave those behind. Come and help me preach The Gospel to all. We need to teach The Word of God to the population.

(John and James look pleased and join the group.)

N	The brothers rushed in great elation. They left their home and in a trice James and John joined Jesus Christ.

(Other disciples join the group.)

N	Soon there were twelve in this growing band. For the next three years throughout the land,
N	They trekked to every village and town, Spreading the word of God around.

(Jesus stands in the middle of the stage with the disciples around him and the rest of the class sit in front as the crowd, listening to him.)

N	The Jews came and listened wherever he went. They said from Heaven he was sent.
N	They preached by the river, and by the seas. They taught with parables and stories.
N	They visited the sick and lame. They healed the dying, the ill and maimed.
N	One day when Jesus preached all day, Andrew said,
Andrew	Shall we send these people away?

	You've preached all day. We all need to eat. Everyone is hungry.
N	Jesus agreed.
Jesus	Find me some food, no matter how small, I can make it last until it's fed all.

(The disciples walk around the crowd on the ground, searching for someone with food. Andrew finds the boy with the loaves and fishes, which he takes to Jesus.)

N	The disciples searched the multitude 'Til they found a child with a little food.
Jesus	Two little fishes and five barley loaves Is more than enough to feed these droves Of hungry people. Tell them all to sit down, While we all bring the food around.

(The rest of the class organize themselves into groups. The disciples mime giving out the food which they mime eating and passing it on.)

N	The multitude sat in groups of fifty. When they heard there was food they moved fairly nifty.
N	The loaves were passed from Jew to Jew. Each piece that was passed, tasted new.
N	The fishes oozed with oil and flesh. After a day in the sun, remarkably fresh.
N	The people ate 'til they were satisfied. All food left-over was thrown aside. Jesus said,
Jesus	I don't like this waste! Pick it up in baskets, just in case, The poor should want it in the town.

(The disciples mime picking up the food.)

N	Andrew and the others walked around, To find all the food and retrieve it! Twelve baskets full! Would you believe it?

(Exit Jesus. The crowd disperses to the back of the stage.)

N	After Jesus was crucified, Andrew went away From Palestine and preached every day.
N	He was Christianity's first missionary. He journeyed round the Mediterranean Sea.
N	He travelled north to Russia, some books say, Teaching the gospel on the way.

(Two children lead Andrew to centre stage and make him stand arms and legs apart, and mime

tying them to a diagonal cross.)

N Sadly our Andrew was crucified.
On a diagonal cross, his body tied.

N He is celebrated in Scotland on 30th November
He is their patron Saint, remember!

N Every year on 30th November, the Scots celebrate St Andrew's day with dancing and singing.

(Children love to sing. There are lots of books around with Scots songs which you can teach them. If you have children in your class learning to play musical instruments or able to do a Scottish dance it is a great opportunity to let them perform.)

Chapter 4 Christian assemblies

St Nicholas' Day

6th December

St Nicholas, the Patron Saint of children and sailors, is better known as Santa Claus. His saint's day is on 6th December, when it is celebrated in other countries. In Britain, the tradition of St Nicholas has become mixed up with the tradition of Father Christmas, the fictitious person, who leaves presents for children on Christmas Day. In spite of his being every child's favourite saint, many know little about St Nicholas.

> **Characters**
>
> St Nicholas
> A poor man
> His three daughters
> Roman soldiers
> Citizens
> All of these, except Nicholas and the poor man, double up as narrators.

N	Good morning and welcome to our assembly.

(Show a large picture of Santa Claus – either on PowerPoint, an OHP picture or even a large piece of wrapping paper.)

> This man is known as Santa Claus or Father Christmas, but many children who wait eagerly for his visit on Christmas Day know little about him. Our class would like to tell you about him.

N	Long ago in the fourth century,
	On the shore of the Mediterranean Sea,
	A thriving city in Southern Turkey
	Basked in Christianity.

(Roman soldiers off-stage. Citizens on stage mingle. Nicholas, wearing a gold cross cut out of card, round his neck, walks around the crowd of people shaking hands, taking out his purse and handing coins to beggars.)

N	In this city of Myra lived Nicholas, a priest.
	His love of his people daily increased.
	This good and kindly Christian leader
	Thought that there was nothing sweeter
	Than to shower his generosity
	On the poor of his lovely coastal city.

N	Each time he heard of someone in need,
	Our Nicholas went at top speed

| | To help them pay their debts and bills.
He protected his people from all ills.
He had kindness no one could surpass
So they made him Bishop Nicholas. |
|---|---|

(Everyone stands back. Nicholas kneels and a child puts a mitre cut out of gold card on a headband onto his head.)

N	But the Roman Emperor ruled supreme.
	Diocletian headed an evil regime,
	It was his burning desire
	To rid the mighty Roman Empire
	Of every trace of Christianity.

(Roman general and soldiers enter. The general stands at the head of two rows of soldiers marching on the spot while the citizens turn their backs and walk away.)

	His soldiers acted without pity.
	Every Christian in every city
	Was thrown into captivity.

N	The people lived in fear and dread
	When a Roman army general led
	His troops into their unhappy town.
	All their shutters were battoned down
	As they waited in fear for the soldiers' knock.

(Two soldiers grab Nicholas and drag him off-stage.)

N	You can imagine the people's shock
	When Nicholas and the other priests
	Were arrested and thrown into jail.
	The citizens began to wail.

1st Citizen	Will we ever again see our priests?

2nd Citizen	Will they ever be released?

3rd Citizen	Have we lost the precious friendship
	Of our dear devoted bishop?

N	Months passed with Nicholas inside.
	But eventually Diocletian died.
	And Constantine the Great took over
	As the first Christian Emperor ever

(Nicholas enters and walks around shaking hands with citizens.)

N	People cheered, their bishop was free
	To shower his generosity
	On all the people whom he loved
	And serve his God in Heaven above.

N	One day Nicholas went out walking.
	And he stopped to listen to people talking.
	They told him of a man in town
	Whose problems were getting him down.

(Nicholas approaches a group of people talking.)

4th Citizen He has a daughter who wants to wed,
But he can't pay her dowry,

N they said.

(They all exit. Nicholas walks around the town until he finds the poor man's house and he quietly opens the window shutters.)

N So late that night when dark came down,
Nicholas walked to the poor end of town.
All was still in the moonlit night.
Our Nicholas stayed out of sight
'Til he was sure they were all asleep.
Up to the poor man's house he creeped.

N He carefully prised the shutters apart
And threw a purse of gold on the hearth.
Then slipped away ever so quick.
Secrecy was important to Nick.

(Nicholas slips away and the poor man appears with three daughters.)

N Next day the poor man opened the door
And found the gold on the living room floor.

Poor man I can't believe it. How can this be?

1st Daughter Someone has left this gold for me!

N The daughter was married with her dowry provided.
At the party, the man proudly presided.

(Poor man and daughter exit. Nicholas approaches a group of citizens who have entered at opposite side.)

N A year later Nicholas was down on the shore.
He sauntered up to a group of the poor.
There was the poor man in the same jam.
His next girl wanted to marry her man.

(The citizens and the poor man exit and Nicholas walks to the house to put a purse of gold in again.)

N So that night again to the rescue came Nick.
With gold in his hand he played the same trick.
He opened the shutters and threw in the gold.
Across the floor coins tinkled and rolled.
The man was delighted, he was over the moon.

(Exit Nicholas. Enter poor man with two daughters.)

Poor man My goodness!

N he said,

2nd Daughter

I'll be married soon.

N And once again at the wedding party.
They ate and drank and were happy and hearty.
And of course, a year later, I'm sure you've guessed
The youngest daughter like the rest
Wanted a dowry to be wed.

3rd Daughter Could it possibly happen three times?

N she said.
Nicholas heard of their plight. Would you believe it?
This time the man was waiting to receive it.
He'd sat up each night patiently,
To find the man of generosity.

(Poor man sits waiting. Nicholas approaches quietly.)

N On the third or fourth night he heard quiet feet
Of someone coming down the street.
The footsteps stopped presently
His shutters opened very gently.
At his feet the gold coins landed.

Poor man Who is there?

N the man demanded.
He rushed to the shutter and looked through.

Poor man Oh Bishop, I should have guessed it was you!

N Outside in the street the bishop stood
In his bishop's cloak and belt and hood.
Looking embarrassed as the man sang his praise.
Nick nodded and smiled and went on his way.

(Nicholas smiles and exits.)

N We call Saint Nicholas, Santa Claus.
He is Patron Saint of children and sailors.

N So parents say, each Christmas Eve,
Be good and Santa Claus will leave
Games and books and sweets and toys.
He's the favourite saint of all girls and boys.

(There are songs about Bishop Nicholas on www.stnicholascenter.org which make a lovely finale to this script.)

N Let us pray.
Oh God, thank you for the life of Bishop Nicholas. Help us to be generous and kind like him, and to remember that Christmas is a time for giving and not just thinking about what we want to receive.

Chapter 4   Christian assemblies

Christmas

25th December

A Christmas assembly does not have to be about the traditional Christmas story. In fact pupils and parents like to see an assembly presented from a different angle. It is quite legitimate to take an old idea off the shelf and adapt it.
This adaptation of Dickens' wonderful novel is suitable for a class who are self-disciplined and able to mime and move quickly. Year 5 or 6 might find it fun. Year 3 or 4 might need the actions simplified. It will be a success if you encourage your pupils to make the speeches flow and the movements slick.
Each pupil can have two or three parts giving everyone the opportunity to shine. Costumes and props are unnecessary, although the children will probably want them. I should emphasize to the children that if everyone speaks up and acts well that will make the characters and the story come alive.

Characters

Scrooge
Gentleman collecting for charity
Mince-pie seller
Jacob Marley's ghost
Bob Cratchit
Mrs Cratchit
Tiny Tim
Other Cratchits
Fred, Scrooge's nephew
Fred's wife and guests
Spirit of Christmas Past
Spirit of Christmas Present
Spirit of Christmas Yet to Come
Man and woman in market
Carol-singers, townspeople and narrators who all double up.

N   Good morning and welcome to our assembly. Our form are going to tell you one of England's best loved Christmas stories.

(An active scene. A little group of carol singers are miming carol singing. The mince-pie lady is walking slowly around with her basket of mince-pies. The two smallest children in the class can be playing a game, picking pockets and running away or having a fight (but only if they are really self-disciplined.) People are standing in little groups miming a conversation.)

N   Once upon a time, of all the good days of the year,
           It was Christmas Eve in Victorian times and all were full of cheer.
           The wind was biting hard through dear old London town,
           But hearts were warm and happy, though the snow was trickling down.

Mince-pie seller
Mince pies! Mince pies! Over `ere!

N the mince pie seller cried.

Mince-pie seller
Good `n `ot and tasty. They'll warm you up inside.

Carol singers *(Sung to the tune of 'God Rest You Merry Gentlemen')*
God Rest You Merry Gentlemen, the carol singers sang.
Their voices rose above the wind and distant church bells rang.

Scrooge *(Appears from the back)*
Get out of here you noisy lot!

N angry old Scrooge roared.

Scrooge I'm trying to count my money. Leave my office door!

N A gentleman stepped from the crowd and up to Scrooge's door.

Gentleman *(Approaching Scrooge)*
Mr Scrooge, I want to talk to you. I'm collecting for the poor.
So many people have no food to celebrate the season.
They have no fuel to keep them warm.
We want to stop them freezing.

Scrooge *(In disgruntled mood)*
Are there no workhouses? Are there no jails?
Isn't there room in the poor house if all else fails?
If they can't be bothered to work, they can spend Christmas there.
I don't make merry myself at Christmas. I have no cash to spare.

N Scrooge slammed the door in the kindly gentleman's face.

(A pupil claps his hands loudly to simulate door slamming. Scrooge turns his back and walks off stage. All the street people exit at the other side.)

N He was very shocked and hurt by Scrooge's lack of grace.

(Bob Cratchit and Scrooge enter from the opposite sides of the stage.)

N Scrooge scowled at Bob Cratchit, his timid office clerk.
Who shivered in the office, so cold and bleak and dark.

N Bob wiped his nose, and quivered and coughed.

(Bob looks timid, shivers and wipes his nose.)

Scrooge I suppose that you'll be wanting all of Christmas Day off.

Bob If quite convenient,

N Bob replied.

Bob I'd really like to be
At home all day for Christmas with my wife and family.

Scrooge Oh have it!

N Scrooge grumped as the clock began to chime.

(Child taps six chimes on bell.)

Scrooge Be early in on Boxing Day, to make up for lost time.

(Enter Fred, Scrooge's nephew)

N The office door opened. In stepped a friendly chap.
He tipped the clerk, held out his hand and politely raised his hat.

(Fred shakes hands with Bob and raises his hat.)

Fred Merry Christmas, Uncle Scrooge!

N greeted his nephew Fred.

Fred Come and join us for Christmas dinner,

N the cheerful young man said.

Scrooge Humbug! Christmas is a humbug. I won't celebrate
That stupid nonsense ever again. I think I hate
It more each year. Now get on your way!
I want to count my money. I've been working hard all day.

(Fred and Bob go out. Scrooge follows, mimes locking the door and trudges across the stage, reaches his front door, opens it and gasps.)

N Scrooge trudged home in a miserable mood.
He gasped, for in his hallway stood
A ghastly, sad figure clanking in chains
With a face that was wracked in grief and pain.

N It was the ghost of his dead partner, Jacob Marley.

Marley *(Walks on stage, with a load of paper chains wrapped around him.)*
Listen to me Scrooge, we need a serious parley.
In my life I was never generous or kind.
These dreadful chains are here to remind
Me of the harsh and cruel life I led.
There'll be one for you when your are dead.
Every day your chain's being made.
There's a link for each harsh word you've said.
It will be a long and hefty chain.
You'll carry it forever and suffer its pain.
For your harsh treatment of London's poor,
You will be tortured for evermore.
Three spirits will visit tonight to warn you.
Take their advice, Scrooge. A curse is upon you.

Scrooge Humbug! My eyes and ears are deceiving me.
I'm working too hard! My senses are leaving me!

N He went to bed and slept until one.

(Scrooge lies down. Ghost of Christmas Past enters. Child bangs bell once and Scrooge jumps up.)

And woke with a jolt when a church bell rung.

N	A jolly old spirit before him stood. In a flowing robe with a belt and hood.
Spirit	*(Cheerfully)* Wake up, Scrooge I'm the Ghost of Christmas Past. I'll show you a merry Christmas at last.

(*Ghost of Christmas Past points to two small children smiling and playing happily at the side of the stage.*)

N	He showed him a happy little girl and boy. A distant Christmas full of love and joy. Scrooge was the boy with his sister Fanny, Spending Christmas at home with a happy family.

(*Children walk off and Mr Fezziwig and another group comes on at the other side. Scrooge hangs his head in shame.*)

N	Scrooge's face fell and his eyes filled with tears. He hadn't been kind to a child for years. And another party the spirit showed Where laughter resounded and the hot punch flowed.
N	Mr Fezziwig, the boss, gave the office party. All ate and drank and felt hale and hearty. Scrooge, the young clerk joined in the fun. They sang and danced 'til the clock struck one.

(*The Fezziwig party mime eating and drinking, chatting and laughing and walk off.*)

N	Scrooge hung his head when he remembered the day. He had treated them all in a miserable way.

(*Spirit walks off and Scrooge lies down*)

> The Spirit of Christmas Past led him home
 To wait for the next Christmas Spirit to come.

(*Child strikes bell twice*)

N	At two, Scrooge woke with a terrible start. The sight of the ghost sent a shot through his heart.
Spirit	I'm the Spirit of Christmas Present,
N	he said.
Spirit	We have places to go. Hurry out of that bed!
N	They sped through the night 'til they came to the home Where Fred had invited old Scrooge to come. The family were gathered and love filled the air. Scrooge realised what he was missing there.

(*Fred, his wife and a few others enter, miming laughing and chatting.*)

N	Scrooge wished he could dine with Fred and his wife. He was suddenly ashamed of his miserable life.

(*Fred's party exit and the Cratchits enter.*)

N	The Spirit lifted Scrooge high off the ground. Over chimneys and trees to the poor end of town. A different party was in full swing. Bob Cratchit's large family were partying.

(*The Cratchits are hugging and kissing and wishing each other a merry Christmas.*)

N	The family had travelled through blustery weather To celebrate Christmas and make merry together. Tiny Tim, his youngest, a small, sickly boy Was laughing heart'ly full of Christmas joy.
N	Bob lifted a glass when the family were fed,
Bob	Let's drink a toast to us all, and to Scrooge,
N	he said.
Mrs Cratchit	That miserable skinflint! Why drink to his health? So mean and so greedy, though loaded with wealth!
N	Said his wife in disgust,
Mrs Cratchit	Let's forget him today!
Bob	Bless us all!
N	replied Bob in his jovial way.
Tiny Tim	God bless us every one,
N	chimed Tiny Tim. Scrooge blushed with shame as he looked at him. The Spirit of Christmas frowned at the miser.
Spirit	I hope these scenes will make you wiser.

(*Scrooge hangs his head and takes out a handkerchief to wipe his eyes, walks away and lies down to wait for the next ghost.*)

N	Back over chimneys and trees they both flew. Scrooge, heart-broken, didn't know what to do. His heart was a stone pressing hard in his chest. The Cratchits so poor, yet so happy, so blest.
N	And Scrooge so wealthy but so sad and so poor. Shaking and trembling he waited for The Spirit of Christmas Yet to Come. The church clock struck - bong, bong, bong.

(*Child bangs bell three times. Enter third spirit.*)

N	The dark spirit smelled of disease and death. Scrooge's heart missed a beat and he held his breath. The spirit loomed over him and pointed the way. Scrooge, terrified, could only obey.

(*The market. Some people standing behind a table miming holding up things to sell while others looked on interested.*)

N	He showed Scrooge a scene of a market stall. The trader was laughing and displaying all Her best quality merchandise. Scrooge was aghast for he recognised His own curtains and clothes on the market stand.
Woman	Thank goodness he is gone, that hideous man! I grabbed what I could when I heard he was dead.
Man	We're all 'appier without him,
N	the trader said.

(*The market people exit and the Cratchits enter, heads bowed in silence*)

The spirit led Scrooge to the church graveyard.
A tearful family was staring hard
At a little grave with flowers dressed,
Where Tiny Tim Cratchit had been laid to rest.

(*Exit Cratchits, heads bowed*)

N	Overwhelmed with remorse, Scrooge fell on his knees.
Scrooge	(*Kneeling*) Kind Spirit, forgive me. Help me please, Don't let this happen. Let me make amends. I'll be kinder. I will change, before my life ends. Could these people ever love me? Could they ever forgive? Show me how can I stop this and make Tiny Tim live?

(*Scrooge lies down and Spirit exits*)

N	The Spirit wouldn't answer. He walked into the night, Leaving Scrooge in his horror, sadness and fright.
N	Next morning Scrooge woke at the crack of dawn.

(*Scrooge wakes up and dresses excitedly*)

Excited and happy he put his best suit on.
He bought the biggest turkey that he could see
And sent it to the Cratchit family.

N	He joined his nephew, Fred, for dinner With the humility of a sorry sinner. He gave Bob Cratchit much better pay And greeted him kindly every day.

(*All of the characters come on stage in groups. Scrooge walks around shaking hands miming convivial conversation.*)

N	He became a second father to Tiny Tim. (*Tiny Tim hugs Scrooge*) And every Christmas it was said of him He kept Christmas faithfuly, and lived every day In a humane and kindly way.

N   He was friendly and cheerful and joined in the fun
                   And his clients blessed him, everyone.

Whole class cheers.

N   Let us pray.
                   Oh God, thank you for the gift of Christmas. Help us all to keep the spirit of Christmas alive this year, to be generous to people who are less comfortable than ourselves and to be kind in all our dealings with others.

Chapter 5 Hindu assemblies

Ganesh Chaturthi

August/September

At the festival of Ganesh Chaturthi, Hindus celebrate the life of the God, Ganesh. If you have Hindus in your class, they may be able to perform a song or a dance of their own culture. I have found that they are often delighted to dress up in their national costume and perform. Parents are often very eager to support teachers in this way and they appreciate their own culture being positively acknowledged.

> **Characters**
>
> Shiva, Ganesh's father
> Parvati, Ganesh's mother
> Ganesh
> An elephant
> Lots of narrators

N   Good morning parents, this week, Hindus celebrate the life of the Hindu God Ganesh. Our class are going to tell you his story.

N   The story of Ganesh
In India thousands of years ago,
Where the mountain range is capped with snow,
The Himalayas stood majestically
And were home to Shiva and Parvati.

(*Shiva and Parvati wander across the stage, holding hands, and looking at each other affectionately.*)

N   Shiva was a god of wisdom and stature.
Parvati, his wife, loving and demure.

(*Shiva holds his head up and his shoulders back looking important, while Parvati smiles up at him, fluttering her eyelashes and stroking his cheeks.*)

       They lived together in peace and love
And surveyed their kingdom from the peaks above.

(*They both look around, satisfied with the surroundings.*)

N   Shiva was a thinker, intelligent and great.
He loved to go off and meditate.
And much as he loved his gorgeous wife
He wanted a bit of space in his life.

(*Shiva gives Parvati a hug, waves good-bye to her and exits while she takes out her handkerchief and mimes crying.*)

N He often left her at home on her own,
While he went off to think alone.
Into the mountains he would go and stay.
While Parvati was lonely every day.

Parvati (*In a disgusted tone of voice*)
What's the point of being a goddess
Living in luxury and great finesse?
If I'm bored and lonely for years at a time.
I should be living it up while I'm in my prime!
I know what I'll do. I'll make a baby.
That will make me happy. Maybe,
Shiva will be pleased when he will come
Back to our palace and stay at home.

(*Parvati exits and returns carrying a washing up bowl covered with brown sugar paper to make it look like pottery, with a doll inside it, and begins miming clay and water modelling.*)

N She chose a dish the next sunny day
And gathered some earth and water and clay.
She mixed them together and rolled it around
And turned it out on a sheet on the ground.

N Then she started to push and press and scrape
The soft clay into a beautiful shape.
She formed a body creatively
And smoothed the skin so delicately.

N A head and a body and legs appeared.
Thrilled with her baby Parvati cheered.

(*Parvati cheers and lifts up her doll and continues shaping its features.*)

She carefully shaped the fingers and toes
And eyes and ears and mouth and nose.

N She carried it down to the holy water   (*Picks it up and carries it*)
And wondered,

Parvati Do I want a son or a daughter?
A son, I think, might please my Shiva.

N She sprinkled him with water from the Ganges river.

(*Mimes sprinkling on the water*)

The holy water did the trick
He came alive and began to kick
His little feet and laughed and cried.

N Parvati delighted was beside
Herself with happiness. (*Skips around the stage cradling her doll.*)

Parvati (*To the audience*)
There is some point to being a goddess!

N The water and clay were blood and flesh.
She called her lovely child Ganesh.
She took him home and fed him and dressed him.
Loved and adored him, cuddled and blessed him.

(*She mimes the motherly actions.*)

N And every day the goddess and son
Spent many hours having fun.
She taught him to love and play and talk
And every day they took a walk.

(*Parvati carries her doll off-stage.*)

N The pair were so happy the years just flew.
And every year young Ganesh grew.

(*Parvati walks back on holding hands with child as Ganesh.*)

One hot summer day the pair were walking through
A mountain wood enjoying the view.

N They came upon a deep blue pool.
The water was fresh and clean and cool.

Parvati I'd love a swim. This pool looks good.
Keep guard by that tree while I'm in the nude.

(*Exit Parvati. Ganesh stands guard.*)

N Ganesh waited while Mum had a swim.
Along came Shiva, all neat and trim. (*Enter Shiva*)

Ganesh You can't go there!

N Ganesh told him fast.

Shiva You can't stop me. I will go past!

N Shiva, incensed, disliked his tone.
He hated boys with a mind of their own.

Shiva Out of my way or take the consequences.

N Poor little Ganesh was quite defenceless.
He wouldn't move. Shiva saw red.
A swish of his sword removed Ganesh's head.

(*Shiva mimes swishing off Ganesh's head, possibly with a plastic sword. Ganesh falls down dead. All the children scream.*)

N Parvati heard cries and jumped from the pool.
She saw her child and wailed,

Parvati	You fool! That's our son you have just killed. His innocent blood you have spilled. (*Cries*)
N	Parvati was devastated.
Parvati	You killed the son that I created!
Shiva	I'll bring our son back to life. Anything to please my wife.
N	Shiva, distraught and horrified Strode quickly down the mountainside. (*Strides across the stage*) He found an elephant by a tree.

(*Shiva approaches a child on all fours with an elephant mask.*)

Shiva	I can take his head, usefully.

(*He swishes plastic sword at elephant who falls down, removes the mask and carries it to Ganesh and places it over his head and breathes on him.*)

N	He swished it off and carried it home And joined it to the body of his lifeless son. He breathed on the body his divine breath And that soon put an end to death.
N	Her son alive, Parvati was delighted. At last her family was united!

(*The three stand up together and everyone in the class cheers.*)

N	Let us pray. Oh God, whichever faith we have, help us always to look after our own families and friends. For a Hindu festival it is appropriate to ask the Hindu children to say or sing a prayer suitable for the festival of Ganesh.

Chapter 5 Hindu assemblies

Divali

October/November

Divali is one of the most important Hindu festivals. It is also celebrated by Sikhs and Jains. It is a time of joy and the Hindus celebrate with fireworks and putting candles in their windows to remind them that people in Ayodhia put lights out to show Rama and Sita the way home.

> **Characters**
>
> King Dasratha
> Rama, Bharat, Lakshman, Shatrughan, his sons
> Kausalya, Kaikei, Sumitra, his wives
> Hanuman, the monkey king
> Sita, a beautiful princess
> A troop of monkeys
> Ravana, an evil ten-headed demon who wants to kidnap Sita
> Maricha, Ravana's supporter who turns himself into a golden deer
> A band of demon supporters
> Narrators
>
> (*Bharat, Shatrughan, the wives, monkeys and demon supporters double up as narrators.*)

N　　　　　Good morning and welcome to our assembly. This week Hindus, Sikhs and Jains are celebrating Diwali. We would like to tell you the exciting story of Rama and Sita.

(*The class can stand in an arc at the back of the stage and step forward to play their part at appropriate times or wait off-stage.*)

N　　　　　In an ancient Kingdom in India's north
　　　　　　Lived a goodly king of wisdom and worth.
　　　　　　From his palace his good name went forth.

(*Dasratha struts across stage, upright and proud.*)

N　　　　　The fine buildings and temples of Ayodhia
　　　　　　Were the pride of beautiful India.
　　　　　　And in that distant, foreign clime
　　　　　　King Dasratha ruled sublime,
　　　　　　With his wives and sons in a prosperous time.

(*Two wives, Kausalya and Sumitra, and four sons walk towards him looking at him happily. The other wife Kaikei looks at Rama in annoyance.*)

N	Happy in a magnificent, regal palace, Furnished with plate and silver chalice, He was unaware of his second wife's malice.

(*The wives stand aside and the four sons start playing and Dasratha looks on fondly.*)

N	Dasratha dearly loved each son, Rama, Bharat, Lakshman and Shatrughan They spent each day having fun.

(*Each son in turn looks towards his father and acknowledges his name. One son falls while playing and Rama helps him up.*)

N	Dasratha watched his fine sons growing, Rama the eldest was always showing Qualities of character and kindness.

(*Sita walks up to Rama who leaves the group to take her arm and they smile at each other and walk away together.*)

        And he married Sita, a beautiful princess.

(*Enter Queen Kaikei*)

N	But Queen Kaikei couldn't stand it. She went to her husband and demanded,

(*The sons and Sita move away and Kaikei approaches Dasratha.*)

Kaikei	You remember the day I saved your life? When you were sinking in the battle's strife.
Dasratha	Of course I remember, my darling wife.
Kaikei	You promised me that day that you would grant Me a wish. Anything I want.
Dasratha	You can have anything you want. You know a king cannot recant On a promise. My queen can demand. Speak out Kaikei. Your wish is my command.
Kaikei	Send Rama away for fourteen years,
N	she said.
Kaikei	Let my son Bharat rule next instead.
N	Dasratha was aghast. This broke his heart.

(*Dasratha turns his back on Kaikei who walks away. Rama enters from the other side.*)

N	He went to Rama to impart The dreadful news of his dear son's fate. He was stunned by the depth of his young wife's hate. But Rama was an honourable, obedient lad.
Rama	A promise must be kept, however bad The consequences. I'll go away for fourteen years. The time will pass and I'll come back here.

N	Sita, his wife, insisted on going Into the forest with Rama, showing Her devotion. And Lakshman also joined the pair. Shatrughan sank into despair.

(Sita and Lakshman join Rama on stage.)

N	So Rama and Sita kissed all good-bye. The loss of his sons made Dasratha cry. The trio got their things together And stepped out of the kingdom to face the weather.

(The trio hug, kiss and shake hands with all the family except Kaikei and leave.)

N	Bharat was sad to lose his brothers. He was so angry with his mother.
Bharat	To remind us the true heir is Rama alone, I'll keep his slippers by the throne.

(The family go off and Rama, Sita and Lakshman re-enter.)

N	Deep in the jungle they found a clearing And built a home, all the time fearing An attack of animals or demons and things And bustling creatures with horns and wings.

(They mime building and going inside the shelter and lying down.)

N	The shelter was made and inside they crept. Exhausted by it all, they soundly slept. 'Til morning when they woke and Rama said,
Rama	We're going hunting, you stay in bed. We'll draw a magic circle all around So you can stay here safe and sound.

(They go out. Ravana enters and looks across at Sita, who eventually gets up and makes herself busy.)

N	Outside their makeshift home there lurked An evil demon while Sita worked. Ravana, this nasty creature, Oozed badness out of every feature. With ten ugly heads and hot red eyes Eager to tempt our Sita with lies, He soon spied Sita, our heroine.
Ravana	Now there's a lady, handsome and fine. And I'm sure that I can convince Her to come with me and leave her prince. She can live in comfort in my castle And escape from all this misery and hassle.
N	He knocked at the door his eyes ablazing. Sita found him shocking and amazing.

(*Sita looks at Ravana and is shocked.*)

Ravana Come pretty princess and join me today.

Sita NO!

N shrieked Sita,

Sita GO AWAY!

(*Sita turns away*)

N Ravana was not dismayed
In the jungle all day he stayed.
Dreaming up a fiendish plan
To steal our princess from her man.
He went and found his friend Maricha.

Ravana I have a plan. I want to reach a
Beautiful princess and tempt her away.
To my castle and make her stay.
Turn yourself into a golden deer.
Skip through the jungle and then appear
At Sita's hut and we'll try to coax
Her away with a little hoax.

N So Maricha turned himself into
A golden deer and darted through
The jungle until he found their home.
And waited for them all to come.

(*Rama and Lakshman return. Maricha who has taken the form of a golden deer enters and passes by. He is on all fours.*)

N He sat down gently on the grass.
Sita came out of the hut at last.
She saw the deer and her heart was struck.
By his peacefulness. The demon was in luck.

Sita Oh look there, Rama, a golden deer.
I'd love to stroke him. Bring him here. (*Exit Maricha*)

N The golden deer suddenly fled.
Rama chased him but Lakshman stayed. (*Rama follows Maricha*)
Eventually Rama shot the deer
And the golden creature disappeared.

N And in his place was a hideous demon
Who started yelling and shouting and screaming. (*Cries off-stage.*)
Maricha imitated the voice of the prince.
The cries for help made Sita wince.

Sita Listen to that. My Rama's in danger.
You must go and save him from the stranger.

Lakshman But what about you? I can't leave you alone.

Sita Please go. I'll be quite safe on my own.

Lakshman No one can kill Rama. He is invincible.

Sita But he is crying for help. It's just possible

	He could be killed. Oh please go, Lakshman. Save my Rama, if you can.
Lakshman	I'll draw a magic circle on the ground. Stay inside it. You'll be safe and sound. (*He exits*)
N	Sita waited anxious and scared. By all the yelling and crying she heard. Ravana went to her in disguise. With a gentle voice and kindly eyes In a saffron robe that's worn by monks. And Sita was fooled by him at once.
Ravana	What is wrong? Why are you worried?
Sita	I wanted the deer so Rama hurried Into the jungle to find him for me. We heard cries and I made Lakshman go. I'm terrified and desperate to know What has happened to Rama and Lakshman.
N	Come with me. I'll help you find them. Desperate to see her Rama, she wept And out of the magic circle she stepped.

(*Narrator clashes a cymbal.*)

N	In a blinding flash he was transformed Into the demon all horrid and horned. Ravana leapt with a cheer of delight And carried Sita off into the night.

(*Ravana grabs Sita who is terrified and cries.*)

N	His chariot lifted them into the sky And Sita, terrified, started to cry.
Sita	Where are you taking me? I want my Rama. You'll never change me with this drama.
Ravana	You be my wife. You'll stay with me!
Sita	Oh no I won't. That could never be. Where are we going? Set me free!
Ravana	Far away, my love! The forest is behind you. In my castle in Lanka, Rama'll never find you. He can search forever and a day, But in my castle you will stay.
N	His chariot soared higher and higher O'er hill and mountain, ocean and fire Until it landed on Lanka's fields And Sita's fate seemed horribly sealed.

(*Ravana and Sita go off. Enter Rama and Lakshman.*)

N	Meantime our princes saw the trick. With hearts a-thumping rushed back quick

	Terrified to their little home. They called for Sita but she did not come.
N	They searched the forest the hills and dales. They searched by the river and mountains and vales. They sat down shattered, anxious, distraught.

(*They mime searching*)

Rama and Lakshman
    She must have been carried away,

N	they thought. They visited Hanuman, the monkey king. They asked if he could do anything To help find Sita and bring her home.

(*They approach Hanuman who enters stage wearing a monkey mask.*)

Hanuman	Leave it to me. My monkeys roam Along every coast on the Indian Ocean. You know lads I have a notion. The demon Ravana was seen Last night in his chariot with your lovely queen.
N	The magic monkeys searched lowlands and highlands Until at last they reached Lanka island.

(*Monkeys search off and on stage*)

    And there on the castle parapet
    Stood a terrified princess, in a sweat.

(*Sita re-enters looking distressed*)

N	The monkeys secretly spied The lovely Sita as she sat and cried. Back they rushed to Hanuman.

(*Enter Rama, Lakshman, Hanuman*)

Monkey	She's on the island. Let's get the band Of monkeys armed and in the mood For a right old fight to free the good And kindly Princess Sita. Let's get that Ravana and beat him!
N	And so they made a bridge to cross The Indian Ocean without loss Of life. They made it To the island and they raided The demon's castle and found the girl. Ravana was in a whirl.

(*Each monkey pairs up with a demon supporter and they mime fighting in pairs. Emphasize that no child actually touches another. Rama and Ravana stand at the front of the stage miming fighting as Sita watches.)*

N	Rama fought the demon all day and night Until he killed the monster outright. And the rescued princess shrieked with delight When she saw her prince win the fight.
N	They crossed the ocean once again Leaving the demons silent and slain. And home the band of monkeys led them. Celebrated, wined and fed them.

(The monkeys, Sita and princes mime eating and drinking.)

N	They thanked the brave and clever troop Of monkeys and then left the group. To travel northwards up through India Towards the lovely home in Ayodhia.

(They shake hands with the troop of monkeys who exit and then they start walking.)

N	Fourteen years slowly slipped away Until at last came the day, The trio approached the mountain kingdom Where the temple bells were loudly ringing.

(Bells ring)

N	Dasratha had long since passed away. And as the trio passed along the day, People lit candles to show the way. Back in the palace they were welcomed home Never more from his kingdom to roam.

(Bharat, Shatrughan, Kausalya and Sumatra welcome them home with hugs and kisses.)

Prayer

As with the assembly on Ganesh, some Hindu, Sikh or Jain children might like to sing or say an appropriate prayer, or children might write their own or use this one.

N	Let us pray. Oh God help us to avoid being jealous or behaving spitefully towards others. Instead help us always to be willing to help others.

Chapter 6   Jewish assemblies

Purim - the Story of Esther

March

The story behind the festival of Purim is in the Old Testament part of the Bible and so it is of interest to Christians as well as Jews. The story of Esther makes a great assembly because it is a story of romance, treachery, danger and good overcoming evil.

> **Characters**
>
> Esther
> Mordecai, her guardian
> Ahasuerus' advisor
> Hegai, servant of Ahasuerus
> Bigthan and Teresh, two treacherous servants of Ahasuerus
> Haman, Ahasuerus' chief minister
> Person at the gate
> Lots of narrators

N   Welcome to our assembly. Each year in March, the Jews celebrate the festival of Purim to commemorate their escape from death. Our form would like to tell you the story of Esther.

N   Five centuries before Christ, in a distant land,
An empire spread across the sand,
From the distant borders of India
To the African land of Ethiopia.

N   This Persian Empire had an almighty king.
He was fabulously wealthy and owned everything.
King Ahasuerus had his palaces adorned
With marble and silver and precious stones.
He gave banquets for hundreds and how the wine flowed
As they drank from goblets of solid gold.

Advisor   Your Majesty, you ought to have a wife.

Ahasuerus That's a good idea. I haven't had one for a while.

Advisor   Leave it to me. I'll send out a decree in your name that lots of beautiful young women are to be brought to your palace and put into your harem. And when they have had all the beauty treatment, you can choose one.

Ahasuerus That's a brilliant idea. Let it be done.

(*They exit*)

N	So the order went out from the palace in Susa That the king's officers wanted to choose a Beautiful maiden fit to be queen. They found the loveliest girls ever seen.
N	Now Mordecai, a good Jewish man Had an adopted daughter and a plan.

(*Enter Mordecai and Esther*)

Mordecai	Esther, the Emperor is searching for a beautiful young woman to be his wife.
Esther	But he won't want me. I'm a Jewish girl.
Mordecai	He doesn't know that we are Jewish. We have had a hard life. We were carried away from our home in Jerusalem when we were attacked. I shall take you to the King's palace and we'll see if they like you. We will not tell them that we are Jewish.
Esther	I'm rather frightened.
Mordecai	Don't be afraid, because I'm sure God will look after us both.
N	So Esther was taken to the palace next day, And introduced to the servant Hegai.

(*Enter Hegai*)

Hegai	This is a very attractive woman. She can join the harem and we will give her all the expensive beauty treatments to make her fit to be a queen.
Mordecai	Goodbye, Esther. Don't be afraid. I shall come to the palace gates often to hear news of you.
Esther	Goodbye Mordecai. (*She kisses him good-bye and he exits*)

(*Esther mimes combing her hair, putting on cream, sleeping.*)

N	Now life in the palace for Esther was good. She had perfumes and creams and plenty of food. A comfortable place to sleep at night. For a while it seemed life was turning out right.
N	After a year of comfort and ease It was Esther's turn to try to please King Ahasuerus. He fell for her. And so she became Queen Esther.
N	Now Mordecai often walked around The iron gates of the palace ground. One day when he was out walking He heard some angry servants talking.
Bigthan	I am annoyed with the king. He never treats us fairly.
Teresh	I am as well. The king never shows us favour.
Bigthan	I want to kill Ahasuerus.
Teresh	We can do it at night when he is sleeping.

(*They move away. Esther enters.*)

Esther   Hello Mordecai. I'm so pleased to see you.

Mordecai   Esther, I am so glad to see you looking so happy, but I have just overheard a terrible conversation. Two of the king's servants, Bigthan and Teresh, are planning to kill him tonight. You must warn him, quickly.

(*Esther rushes off.*)

N   So Esther rushed off and warned the king.
That two servants were plotting this terrible thing.
The men were caught and punished severely.
Ahasuerus was grateful and loved Esther dearly.

N   The king appointed a chief minister named Haman,
A proud and arrogant, nasty man.
And everyone had to bow and scrape
To Haman when he went to the gate.

N   Now Mordecai still came every day
To the gates to hear what they had to say.
When Haman appeared the people bowed low.
But Mordecai turned his back to go.

(*Enter Haman and the person at the gate.*)

Person at the gate
   Why do you not bow to Haman?

Mordecai   Bowing to people is a form of worship. I am a Jew. I only bow to God.

Person   You must be careful. Haman is a very powerful man. If the king hears that you do not bow to his chief minister, you will be in a lot of trouble.

(*Enter Haman. Other person bows but Mordecai walks away.*)

N   Haman came to the gate next day.
He was furious when Mordecai turned away.
A spiteful man he went straight to the king.
And told him that the Jews were plotting.

(*Exit man at gate. Enter Ahasuerus.*)

Haman   Your Majesty there are many Jews in your Empire. They believe that their God is above you and they are refusing to obey your laws. We must kill them all so that everyone must see that no one disobeys the laws of the Persian Emperor.

Ahasuerus   A good idea. Let everyone know that the Jews are to be killed in all parts of my Empire.

(*Exit Haman. Enter Esther.*)

N   And so messengers spread this dreadful news
That Haman was determined to kill the Jews.
The news reached Esther in her palace bedroom.
She planned to save them from their doom.

Ahasuerus   Esther what can I do for you?

Esther	I have a favour to ask of you. Will you and Haman come to have dinner with me tomorrow?
Ahasuerus	Of course, my dear. You will have anything you want.
N	And so the next day, the three of them dined. Haman, full of hatred, was determined To use his power to kill the Jews, And Queen Esther desperate to use Her position to save them all.
Haman	Your Majesty, there is a man at the gate called Mordecai who still refuses to bow.
Esther	But Mordecai was the one who told me of the plot to kill your Majesty. How can he be a traitor?
Ahasuerus	What honour has been given to Mordecai for saving my life?
Esther	None, he has never been rewarded.
Ahasuerus	Then he must have a reward. Now what do you want to ask of me, Esther?
Esther	Ahasuerus, Mordecai is a relation of mine. I am a Jew. Haman wants all of the Jews put to death because one Jewish man refused to bow to him. I ask you to save all the Jews. All these people who would be slaughtered are innocent of any crime against you. Haman has lied to turn you against the Jews.
Ahasuerus	This is an outrage. The order to kill the Jews has already gone out and it cannot be stopped.
Esther	Please allow another to go out allowing the Jews to arm and defend themselves.
Ahasuerus	It must be done at once. See to it now. (*Haman exits, looking angry.*)
N	The order went out and the Jews defended Themselves well, so the danger ended. So Esther managed to save the Jews. Haman almost fainted at the news. He was punished severely for his malice And the king and queen lived long in their palace.

(*Children cheer*)

N	The festival of Purim was started during the life-time of Esther and Ahasuerus. Jews still celebrate it to-day. They go to their synagogues and the story of Esther is read out. Children take whistles and special rattles called greggors and every time the name of Haman is mentioned they make a huge noise to drown out the sound of his name.
N	Sometimes children go to fancy dress parties at Purim and in some Jewish schools they put on a play telling the story. Purim is a time to give money and food to charity.
N	Let us pray. Oh God, we thank you for the many times you have taken an unjust situation and put it right. Help us always to do the right thing even though it is so often easier to do the wrong thing.

Chapter 6   Jewish assemblies

Pesach - The Story of Passover

April/May

Like Purim, this is a Bible story and so it is of interest to the Christian population, particularly because in the days before Easter, Jesus was celebrating Passover the night before he was crucified. This assembly could be used to re-inforce the R.E. unit of Judaism. This script has a lot of action, some of which can be omitted for Lower Juniors.

> **Characters**
>
> Rameses the Pharaoh
> Bithia, Pharaoh's daughter
> Moses
> Jochabed, Moses' mother
> Miriam, Moses' sister
> Slave-master (non-speaking)
> Ruel, Moses' father-in-law (non-speaking)
> Zipporah, Moses' wife (non-speaking)
> Moses' son (non-speaking)
> Voice from the burning bush
> Jews – less than half the class
> Egyptians – less than half the class
> Lots of narrators, who double up with most of the above parts

(*The Jews are on stage in groups, looking happy and content with life, some drinking, some working, some sitting chatting.*)

N   Look back to a few thousand years ago,
             To where the Mediterranean waters flow.
             At the eastern end of the tideless sea,
             The Hebrew people were living free
             In their happy land, in prosperity.

(*They all get into a large group as if discussing what to do and then start moving in a group across the stage and exit.*)

N   For two hundred years the Jews lived in peace,
             But a famine made their fortune cease.
             Hunger spread throughout the land
             Of Canaan. So they travelled across the sand
             To Egypt, a land of drinks and food.
             The Hebrews settled and life was good.

(*Enter Pharaoh*)

N	But the years slipped past and they multiplied, Lived well in Egypt and were satisfied, But Pharaoh watched them with alarm.
Pharaoh	There's too many of them. They could do us harm. If they keep growing at this rate They'll outnumber us and seal our fate. We'll make them slaves. They'll serve us well. Free labour for me. My power will swell.

(*Pharaoh stands front stage at one side and watches the Jews who re-enter, looking unhappy. They mime the heavy labour of building, some pulling heavy weights, some digging, some lifting and carrying.*)

N	And so the Jews were sadly oppressed. God's chosen people were no longer blest. Their faith was now put to the test. In humble, slavish clothes they dressed To build the palaces and cities. For two hundred years their lives were piteous.
Jews	Will no one save us from this life?
N	they cried. But Pharaoh wasn't satisfied For still their numbers multiplied.
Pharaoh	How can it be that there are more Jewish people than ever before? Why does slavery not make them meek? Oppression should make these people weak. But not the Jews, oppressed, they thrive But I'll make sure they don't survive. From now on every Jewish boy Will be killed. That'll end their joy. The girls can live. They are no threat. We'll use them as handy slave-girls yet. Soon their numbers will disappear And Egyptians can live without fear Of being outnumbered.

(*Jews stop work to listen, looking at each other in horror.*)

N	And so the Jews Trembled at this dreadful news. This law set them in a whirl As each prayed their baby would be a girl.

(*Exit Jews and Pharaoh. Enter Jochabed with her daughter, Miriam, a doll and crib. She mimes brushing the outside of the crib with tar and carrying it with the doll to the river.*)

N	A Jewish mother called Jochabed Hid her baby boy in bed Until he was too big to hide. She tarred her crib and laid him inside.

(*Mimes the action of the verse.*)

N	She took him down to the River Nile To hide him in the rushes for a while. Miriam, her daughter, guarded her brother. With the instruction to call her mother If any one should take her brother.

(*Enter Bithia, Pharaoh's daughter*)

N	At last Pharaoh's daughter came to the river. The lovely baby made her quiver With delight.
Bithia	I'll take him and adopt him maybe.
Miriam	I know a woman who could suckle your baby.
N	So Miriam ran to fetch Jochabed.

(*Exit Bithia, Jochabed re-enters*)

Miriam	Princess Bithia has found our baby,
N	she said.
Miriam	I've told her you could be his nurse. Think of it Mother. God has taken the curse Of death away from our family. He'll be safe and sound in the royal palace And still escape the Pharaoh's malice.

(*Exit Miriam and Jochabed*)

N	And so the baby boy became An Egyptian prince, Moses by name. A happy life for him ensued And gradually the baby grew Into a healthy, happy gent.

(*Enter a slave-master and some Jews who mime working. Moses as a young man enters and looks annoyed as he sees the slavemaster beating the Jew.*)

N	But one day as Moses went Along the road where Jewish slaves worked. He saw something that really irked.
N	A slavemaster was beating a slave. Angrily, he took the whip and gave

(*Moses takes the whip and beats the slave-master and drags him off-stage.*)

> The cruel master a hefty lashing.
> The man did not survive the thrashing.

(*Exit slaves*)

N	Moses panicked and buried him in the sand. And terrified he fled from the land.

(Moses rushes in and meets Ruel and his daughter Zipporah.)

> To the land of Midian, Moses ran
> And luckily met a kindly man
> Who gave him shelter, food and a bed.
> Eventually his daughter and Moses were wed.

(Exit Ruel and Zipporah)

(Moses sits on ground looking happily at children who are on all fours as sheep.)

N Now life was comfy for a while,
Away from Egypt, the slaves and the Nile,
With his wife and son. He looked after the sheep
Of his father-in-law to earn their keep.

N This new life was great for him
But back in Egypt, life was grim.
The Hebrews still cried out to God.

Jews *(Off-stage)*
Deliver us from the slave-drivers' rod!

N God heard their cries and looked to Moses
Whose new life was still a bed of roses.
But God had chosen him for the task
Of approaching the Pharaoh to ask
Him to set the Hebrews free
And start a life of liberty.

N Moses saw a bush burning on a hill.
A voice was calling out loud and shrill.
He listened carefully to God's will.

Voice from the bush
Go back to Egypt and speak to Rameses!

N Moses went weak at the knees.

Moses Anything but that, God, please!

Voice Go back to the Pharaoh and ask him to free
My people from their slavery.
Tell him I shall send such devastation
Upon the entire Egyptian nation.
Plague and disease I shall inflict on them
I'll reduce them all to grief and mayhem.

(Enter Zipporah and child. Moses takes leave of them both. They all exit.)

N Summoning his courage Moses went to his wife
To explain God's plan to end the strife
Of Jewish people back in Egypt.
With disappointment she was gripped.

N Her husband leaving, Zipporah wept.
But Moses' promise had to be kept.

(They exit)

> He packed his bag and went to see Rameses

To ask him for a swift release
Of the Hebrew people from slavery.

(*Enter Moses and Pharaoh from different sides.*)

Pharaoh laughed,

Pharaoh How dare you ask that of me!
The slaves will stay and do as I say.
They'll work for me every day.
As long as there's a Jew still standing.
They'll heed all of my commanding.

(*Exit Moses. Enter Egyptians, looking ill, coughing and irritated by mosquitoes etc.*)

N And God sent out the first great plague.
The waters of the Nile he made
Into a sickening river of blood.
Next a plague of frogs began to scud
Across the land, followed by lice.
But Pharaoh would not heed the advice
To release the Jews and avoid the grief.

N From plagues there would be no relief.
Swarms of mosquitoes, gnats and fleas
Invaded Egypt and spread disease.
The farmyard animals were all killed.

N The Egyptians all with anguish filled.
But still the Pharaoh would not budge.
The man was so hardened with a grudge
Full of malice, he could not judge
The full extent of the destruction.
Next there was a black eruption.

(*Moses enters and mimes throwing soot*)

N Moses threw handfuls of filthy soot
Into the breeze to pollute
The air of the entire locality.
Their worst nightmares were now a reality.

N The people all had boils infected.
The hardship made them feel dejected.
In pain and horror they cried,

Egyptians (*Coughing and choking*)
Let them go!

N But still Great Rameses answered,

Pharaoh NO!

N A shower of hailstones covered their fields
But still the Pharaoh would not yield.
Locusts flew in and quickly devoured
All their crops while the Egyptians cowered.

N In three full days without daylight.

                    The Egyptians all had taken fright.
                    In pain and anguish, sorely vexed.
                    They screamed in torment,

Egyptians   Whatever next?

(*Exit some Egyptians. Enter some Jews, who mime painting doorposts to the amusement of Egyptians.*)

N   God's patience now was slipping fast.
                   So next the Hebrews were all asked
                   To paint lambs' blood upon their doorposts.
                   The Egyptians thought it was the most
                   Stupid thing they'd ever seen.
                   But the Angel of Death ruled supreme.

(*All exit*)

N   That night when all were sound asleep.
                   Into every Egyptian house he creeped.
                   A murderous spell was cast upon
                   Every Egyptian first born son.
                   They wept and wailed and clamoured for peace.

(*Enter some Egyptians and Pharaoh*)

Egyptians   Rameses now will you release
                   Us from this life of misery?
                   We've been punished for the life of tyranny
                   That we've inflicted on the slaves.
                   Release them or we'll all be in our graves.

(*Exit Egyptians. Enter Moses.*)

N   Pharaoh wept for his own dead son.
                   His spirit broken, the Jews had won.
                   He answered with a very bad grace.

Pharaoh   Pack your bags and get out of this place!

(*Exit Pharaoh. Enter Jews. They mime eating, drinking, packing and then getting into a crowd and walking on the spot, barefoot so that the narrators can be heard.*)

N   The Jews packed quickly. They dared not wait.
                   For the bread to rise. They swiftly ate
                   Unleavened bread and got on the road.
                   With all their belongings, an enormous load.

N   Hundreds of men with their children and wives.
                   Wondering how they could all survive
                   In the desert with oxen and chickens and cattle,
                   Knowing that now they had to battle
                   Against the hardship of heat and drought,
                   But despair to escape drove them out.

N   They picked their steps o'er the marshy Reed Sea.

(*Exit Jews. Enter Egyptians who march on the spot and eventually fall to the ground, drowned.*)

> The Egyptians followed them desperately
> Anxious to capture and make them return.
> But the Jews were not making any U-turns.
> A horrendous flood swept o'er Pharaoh's men
> Covered their chariots and horses and drowned them.

(*Exit Egyptians*)

N And every year ever since then,
The Jews remember God's goodness to them.

N Each year at Passover they prepare their home
By cleaning each square inch of every room.
Their cutlery and crockery is locked away.
They have special dishes for Passover days.

N Eating leavened bread is abolished.
The candlesticks are carefully polished.
The candles for celebration are lit
And each has a cushion for comfort to sit.

N The Passover meal is specially cooked.
They eat and read from the Hagadah book.
The father starts by giving the blessing
And as they eat they learn the lesson.

N The children ask questions as the meal progresses
And four times they fill their glasses.
They recall the story of the Exodus,
The pain and anguish, the hurry and fuss.

(*Narrators may hold up food as it is mentioned.*)

N And eat food which symbolizes
The different parts of the crisis.
A hard boiled egg for spring and new life.
Bitter herbs remind them of the strife.

N Lettuce to remind them of how life was sweet
Before they were trampled under Pharaoh's feet.
Fresh herbs dipped in salty water
Reminds them of the tears and slaughter.
Haroset reminds them of the mortar
The apples and nuts are mixed like cement
They used for building in the Orient.

N The bones of the lamb which they had to slay
To paint blood on their doorposts that day,
To keep the Angel of Death away.

N And matzah bread crisp and light
Reminds them of the hurry for the flight
From Egypt across the desert sand
To a new life in their promised land.

N And when the meal is nearly done,
The children have a little fun.
Someone has hidden some matzah bread
They search their shelves and cupboards and beds.
And when the matzah has been found

	All the family gathers round The table to have a glass of wine.
N	A glass for the prophet Elijah is poured. The children run and open the door, To see if he is on his way. For the Jews believe he'll return one day.
N	After the Seder meal the celebration goes on Singing the traditional Jewish songs. Psalms of David are sung with delight And the party goes on into the night.
N	Let us pray. Oh God, thank you for saving the Jews so that they could survive and live today. Please look at all oppressed people of the world, especially those who even today are still forced to work as slaves. Please bring slavery to an end and allow all people to live in freedom.

Chapter 6   Jewish assemblies

Shavu'ot - The Giving of the Ten Commandments

May/June

Shavu'ot is the festival which celebrates God giving the Ten Commandments to the Israelites in the desert after their escape from slavery in Egypt. This is a continuation of the assembly script for Passover.

> **Characters**
>
> Moses
> Jews – the rest of the class } These parts double up.
> Narrators   }

(The whole class are spread out on the stage as Jewish people. Moses is at the front.)

N	For two centuries the Jews were gripped In slavery in the kingdom of Egypt. As a saviour from God, Moses was sent And into the desert the Israelites went.
N	There were thousands of Jews, overjoyed to be free, Escaping from hardship and misery, Eager for their first taste of liberty. This great nation, with Moses in command, Desperate to find their Promised Land.
N	But now different problems had begun. How to drink and eat in the desert, for one.
1st Jew	Why have you brought us here? We're dying of thirst!
2nd Jew	Take us back to Egypt. This is worse Than toiling all day in the dust and heat.
3rd Jew	Let us go home. We need to eat.
N	But God heard their cries and desperate pleas And led them to Elim with its springs and trees. Each morning from Heaven came bread like hail And in the evening flocks of quail.

(Jews mime eating and drinking and looking content. They start walking on the spot.)

N	So the Jews moved on through the wilderness But hardship caused them great distress. At times they longed to be settled again, Not constantly walking over bleak terrain.

N	They came to the great Mount Sinai at last. Thunder and lightning and a fierce trumpet blast Shook the mountain and all of the Israelites trembled.
Moses	I want you at the foot of the mountain assembled.
N	The peak was covered in a dark, smoky cloud. The Jews trembled before the deathly shroud. God came down to the top of the mountain And called for Moses to come and meet him.

(*Jews sit down in a bunch and mime chatting discontentedly.*)

Moses	Stay here, everyone, God wants me now.

(*Moses exits*)

N	Moses climbed the mountain and into the cloud He stayed up the mountain for several days. God talked to him about the ways. He wanted his chosen people to live. And the laws that he wanted to give.
N	Meanwhile down at the foot of the hill Where the Israelites were waiting still.
4thJew	What's keeping Moses?
5thJew	Where has he gone?
6thJew	We want to know what's going on.
7th Jew	I'm tired of sitting here, bored out of my brain To spend another day waiting in vain.
8thJew	Life's just a toil!
9th Jew	We never have any fun. We've just waited and walked since this thing's begun.
10th Jew	Let's have a party and let our hair down.

(*They mime the action of the next verses.*)

N	They gathered their jewellery into a big bowl And melted it down to liquid gold. The Jews were artistic, too clever by half, They moulded it into the shape of a calf.
N	They worshipped and danced and partied all night. Moses returned and was furious at the sight.

(*Enter Moses*)

Moses	How dare you worship an idol of gold? How many times have you got to be told? There is only one God in Heaven above! Only one God to worship. Only one God to love!
N	On two tablets of stone he held God's commandments In a fury he smashed them into fragments. And God sent a plague to the Jews as punishment.

N   Now Moses took charge of the people once more
He strictly insisted they keep God's law.
And he led them on across the desert sand
'Til their children arrived at the Promised Land.

N   God's Ten Commandments are: (*Each is said by a different member of the class.*)
1. You will have no other Gods before Me.
2. You must not make any idols and worship them.
3. You must not use my name irreverently to swear.
4. Remember the seventh day is the Sabbath and keep it holy.
5. You must honour your father and mother.
6. You must not kill.
7. You must not steal.
8. You must not leave your husband or wife to go off with someone else.
9. You must not tell lies.
10. You must not be jealous of other people's belongings.

N   The giving of the Ten Commandments is one of the most important events in Jewish history, because it laid down forever the basis of the Jewish Torah.

N   The Ten Commandments are also the basis of Christian law.
The laws of respect for God, honesty and behaviour towards other people are similar throughout other world religions.

N   Today the Jews celebrate Shavu'ot by making their synagogue attractive with flowers because Mount Sinai had flowers on its slopes when Moses went up to talk to God and receive the Ten Commandments. They then have a service in which they read the Ten Commandments.

N   Then they go home to a special meal, which includes bread in the shape of a ladder which represents Moses climbing the mountain to meet God.

N   Let us pray.
Oh God, thank you for teaching us right from wrong and how to behave to please you. Whatever our religion, help us to keep its rules, to put you first, to be honest and considerate of other people.

Chapter 6 Jewish assemblies

Hanukkah

December

Hanukkah is not one of the more important Jewish festivals but as a story of good triumphing over evil it is worth using as an assembly. If you have Jewish children in your class, the parents may be willing to lend you a menorah and a dreidle to show to the school.

> **Characters**
>
> Syrian Emperor
> Mattathias
> Judah Maccabee, Mattathias' son
> Judah's four brothers
> Jewish people
> Greek army officer
> Greeks soldiers
> Narrators who double up with the parts above

(*Start with the Jews, including Mattathias' family, on stage.*)

N   Welcome to our assembly. In December, while most of us are preparing for Christmas, the Jewish people have their own light festival called Hanukkah.

N   Hanukkah means 'dedication'. Our class would like to tell you the exciting story behind the festival of Hanukkah.

N   Imagine the scene in 199BC.
Jews were living in the tyranny
Of another foreign dynasty.

N   The Syrian Empire took over Palestine,
Determined to keep the Jews in line
With their own laws and way of life.
This was bound to lead to strife.

Syrian king   (*At the front*)
We will put an end to Judaism, once and for all!

(*He reads from a scroll. Jews look horrified.*)

> From now on everyone in Israel is forbidden to read the Torah.
> Everyone is forbidden to keep the Sabbath day. Everyone must work on Friday evening and Saturday as normal.
> No one is allowed to circumcise baby boys.
> Pork is not unclean meat and must be eaten by everyone.
> Anyone who does not obey these laws will be punished by death.

(*Exit king*)

N	These laws were read throughout the land. They sent shivers down the spines of every man. How could they bear such oppression From several rulers in succession?
N	And life became worse day after day Their temples were treated in a dreadful way. Pictures and statues of Greek gods were placed In Jewish temples – a terrible disgrace.
1st Jew	These laws are evil. We cannot obey them.
2nd Jew	We must resist them. But how can we keep our own religious ways and escape death for ourselves and our children.
3rd Jew	We must be prepared to practise our religion in secret. One day we will have to stand up for ourselves and fight for our religion and our whole way of life.
N	The years passed and the rulers became more fierce. Determined to have the Greek ways in every place. Antiocchus, a Greek king, in 167BC Ruled his empire with unbearable cruelty.
N	One day his armies marched into Modin. Everyone had a sense of dark foreboding. His army was strong and heavily armed. They didn't care if the people were harmed.
N	Antiocchus was absolutely determined. The whole Jewish creed would be undermined. He sent his soldiers to lots of temples Determined to make harsh examples Of anyone who disobeyed Greek rules.
N	Would anyone dare? They'd be fools To fight such an army. They couldn't possibly win. One brave old Jew thought it a sin To accept the Greek way of life, And he was willing to enter the strife.

(*Mattathias, his sons and others are in the street. Greek soldiers enter.*)

Greek army officer
From now on you will worship Zeus and the other Greek gods.
Statues of Greek gods will be placed in every temple.
All Jewish traditions must stop at once.
Anyone who disobeys the laws of Antiocchus will be put to death.

4th Jew (*Frightened*)
All right, we'll accept the Greek way of life.

(*The Greeks exit*)

Mattathias That's an evil thing to do. We can never give up our Jewish way of life or worship false gods.

(*He takes out a plastic knife/sword, stabs him and speaks to the others.*)

	We must never give in to the Greeks. We must be prepared to arm ourselves and fight them. It would be better to be dead than to live under Greek laws and the Greek way of life.
5th Jew	Mattathias, is there any chance we could win? They are a very powerful army and they outnumber us.
Mattathias	We must trust in God. He will protect us and help us to overcome our enemies. Who will join me and my sons and stand up to the Greeks?
All the others (*Raising hands in support*)	We will join you. / We'll fight the Greeks. / We'll stand up to them.

(*Except for a few narrators, the whole class now divides into two groups, one Jewish, one Greek. They face each other across the stage and mime a battle scene, as a background to the following verses. Each Jew can pair up with a Greek and work out their own fight motions. They can use plastic swords and shields if they wish, but the action is mimed and they may not touch each other. It is easier if it is done in slow motion.*)

N	Mattathias' five sons gathered their troops. They armed themselves and got into groups. Led by Judah Maccabee, the most famous son, They gathered strength and everyone Was ready to fight 'til the war was won.
N	Maccabees means men as strong as hammers, Ready to enter the battle clamours. Talk of rebellion now was rife. The Jews would fight for their way of life.
N	With God on their side they kept their nerve. They fought with courage and strength and verve. Outnumbered, they never feared to lose For God would not desert the Jews.
N	They were ready to fight for as many weeks As it took to defeat the warring Greeks. For two whole years the war was waged With courage and fierceness the battles raged.
N	And every time the armies engaged Whatever the danger the Jews battled. At last the Greeks were getting rattled. Though greater in size they were frightened to meet them. At last the Jews managed to defeat them.

(*The Greeks are now on the floor, injured and beaten, and the Jews are standing and cheering.*)

Judah	We have won. We are free men again. Let's go to the temple and give thanks to God for our victory.

(*The Greeks stand up and exit.*)

N	Off to the temple to worship and pray. For giving them the victory that day. The Jewish people worked quite slickly. The Greek idols were thrown out quickly.
Judah	We now have to rededicate our temple to God. Has anyone found the menorah?

1st Brother	I have found the menorah, but is there any oil for it?
2nd Brother	There is only enough oil for one evening. We really need a lot more.
Judah	I'll go off to get some but I don't think I can get back for several days. That oil will have burnt out before I return.
2nd Brother	It doesn't matter. Just go anyway and we'll fill it up when you return.
N	So off went Judah while the others concentrated On preparing the temple to be rededicated. Greek pictures and statues were gleefully destroyed. A task, I should think, the Jews enjoyed.

(*They mime the verse*)

N	From top to bottom the temple was cleaned Till every wall and window gleamed. For eight days they waited 'til Judah returned, And still the oil lamp in the temple burned.
Judah	This is a miracle, a sign from God. He has kept the oil burning for eight whole days. We must give thanks to God.
N	Today Jewish people commemorate the miracle by lighting eight candles on a special candlestick called a menorah. A menorah has eight candles of the same height in a line. The ninth is called the Shamesh and it is placed in the middle. It is taller and it is used to light the others.
N	On the first night they light the candle on the left of the menorah with the Shamesh. They then say three blessings.
N	Blessed are you Adonai, Ruler of the World, who has kept us alive and well, and brought us to this season.
N	Blessed are you, Adonai our God, Ruler of the World, who makes us holy through your mitzvoth, and commands us to kindle the Hanukkah lights.
N	Blessed are you, Adonai our God, Ruler of the World, who worked miracles for our ancestors in days long ago, at this season.
N	On the second night they light two candles, starting with the new candle and then the first one again, three on the third until the eighth night when all are lit.
N	Jewish families then sing Hanukkah songs like 'Rock of Ages' and 'These Lights' to celebrate the miracle.
N	At Hanukkah people eat foods fried in oil as a reminder of the miracle of the oil lasting for eight days. Children get presents at Hanukkah and play games. One of their favourite games is the dreidle game.
N	To play it you need a four-sided top called a dreidle. (*Hold one up to show, if you can borrow one from a Jewish family.*) It has a Hebrew letter on each side, nun, gimmel, heh and shin. (*Show them in turn.*) Each child starts with ten pence or chocolates and they start by putting one into the pot in the middle. They spin the top in turn and if it stops at nun, they do nothing. If it stops at gimmel, the player wins the pot. If the dreidle stops on heh, the player takes half the pot and if it lands on shin the player adds two to

the pot. Every time the pot is empty, each has to add one item to the pot.
The game is over when one player owns all of the items.

N   Let us pray.
Oh God, thank you for the many times you have helped people of all religions. Help us always to be willing to reach out and help others as you have helped the Jews.

Chapter 7 Muslim assemblies

Birthday of the Prophet Muhammad, (PBUH)

12th day of Rabi-al-Awwal

Muhammad, as Prophet of the Islam, is a greatly revered person to the Muslims. They like to add 'Peace be upon him' to his name. This is normally shortened to 'pbuh'. The birthday of the prophet Muhammad, (pbub), is a very important celebration to the Muslim population. It is celebrated on the 12th day of Rabi-al-Awwal, the third month of the Islamic calendar and so is on a different date on the Gregorian calendar, every year.

Characters

Muhammad (pbuh)
Muhammad's uncle
Khadija, Muhammad's wife
Angel Gabriel
People in the crowd
Narrators
Friend

(*All of the class on stage*)

N	Welcome to our assembly. This week, Muslims will be celebrating the birthday of Muhammad (pbuh).
N	Who was Muhammad, (pbuh)?
N	Muhammad, (pbuh), was the Prophet of Islam.
N	What does Islam mean?
N	Islam means 'peace and giving in to the will of God'. This morning we would like to tell you about the Prophet Muhammad, (pbuh), and how he started the great religion of Islam.
N	Muhammad, (pbuh), was born in Makkah in 571AD which is in Saudi Arabia. He was member of the Quraysh clan. They were an important family who had organized the city of Makah.
N	One of their tasks was to look after the huge, black, cuboid-shaped shrine called the Kaaba.
N	At that time, people worshipped many idols. Some people say that at the time of Muhammad's youth, there were 360 idols in the Kaaba.
N	When he was a young boy, Muhammad, (pbuh), did not like many of the things he saw, and he spent a lot of time thinking about them and wondering what he could do about it all.

(Muhammad, (pbuh), as a boy, is out walking with his uncle. Two children mime a man beating a slave.)

Muhammad Why is he beating that young boy?

Uncle That young boy is his slave. He can do what he wants with him.

Muhammad But why is he beating him?

Uncle He probably did not do his work well enough.

Muhammad But that's dreadful, Uncle. Surely one person cannot be allowed to own another. How can anyone be so cruel as to beat a young boy? Can't anyone do anything to stop them?

Uncle It has always happened, Muhammad. I don't think anyone could stop it.

(Muhammad, (pbuh) and his uncle go on walking and stop when they see children miming praying to idols)

Muhammad What are those people doing, Uncle?

Uncle They are saying their prayers. They pray to those little statues.

Muhammad But why Uncle, they are only made of wood. They are not real gods who can help people.

Uncle Well I suppose people like to think they can help them.

Muhammad Uncle, look at those people over there. They are throwing a baby away. How can they do something so cruel?

(Children walking along with an unbreakable doll. They throw it off-stage.)

Uncle The baby belongs to a slave. They don't want it because it's a girl. That's why they are throwing it away.

Muhammad But the slave girl might want it. This is awful, Uncle. Someone ought to stop this cruelty.

N Muhammad, (pbuh), was very worried about all these things happening and he often thought about it. As he got older, everyone who knew Muhammad, (pbuh), had respect for him.

(Uncle exits and a group of children gather round Muhammad, (pbuh))

Muhammad *(To the group)*
You know, there are so many things which people do that are wrong. No one has any right to beat a slave. They have as much right to be treated kindly as anyone else.

Friend Not everyone believes in being as kind as you, Muhammad, or as honest. You deserve your nickname, Al-Amin, the honest one.

Muhammad Somehow we must one day change things so that everyone treats everyone else fairly.

N Time went on and eventually when Muhammad, (pbuh), was twenty-five he married Khadija.

(Khadija enters and walks up to Muhammad. They smile at each other and link arms.)

N They were happy together and had several children. However Muhammad, (pbuh), was still unhappy about the way people lived and behaved. He used to go up into the mountains to think about it and he kept wondering what he could do to stop people behaving badly.

(*Everyone exits and Muhammad, (pbuh), walks up into the mountains.*)

N One day in the year 610 AD, when Muhammad, (pbuh), was almost 40 years old, he went up into the mountains to be alone so that he could think. He was visited by the Angel Gabriel.

Muhammad Who are you?

Gabriel I am the Angel Gabriel, God's messenger. God has asked me to tell you that he does not like the people of Makkah behaving badly. You must be the one to tell them to stop worshipping idols. They must worship the one true God. You must tell them to stop killing baby girls and treat all people kindly.

Muhammad But how can I do that?

Gabriel You must remind them of the word of Ibrahim, Moses and Jesus Christ. God is angry that people have ignored his laws. You must be the one to bring them back to His way of life.

Muhammad But will they listen to me? Will they believe me?

Gabriel God will help you. Go down from the mountain and start God's work.

(*Exit Gabriel. Muhammad (pbuh), starts walking home.*)

Khadija Muhammad, I'm glad you are home again. Do you feel better after your rest in the mountains?

Muhammad You'll never believe who came to visit me in the mountains. The Angel Gabriel. He told me to be God's next Prophet on Earth. I have to go round Makkah telling every one to stop worshipping idols and only worship the one true God. I have to tell people to stop killing baby girls and treating slaves cruelly.

Khadija But this is what you want to do, Muhammad. Now that you have God's blessing, he will help you.

N So Muhammad, (pbuh), began to preach the Word of God. Many people did not like it.

Muhammad (*Standing in front of the class who form a crowd*)
God has sent me to warn you. We must remember the word of Ibrahim and stop worshipping false gods.

1st Person in the crowd
Why? You can't tell us what to do.

Muhammad It is wrong to keep slaves and beat them cruelly.

2nd Person in the crowd
Why? We have bought them. We can do what we like with them. They make us a lot of money. I think we should keep them.

Muhammad No one has the right to own anyone else or treat them cruelly. God has sent his Angel Gabriel to tell you all that if you continue to disobey God's laws you will never get to Paradise to be with him.

3rd Person in the crowd
>And what is Paradise like?

Muhammad Paradise is where people who have kept God's law go to when they die. It is a land of gardens where everything grows. There is plenty of food and drink and everyone lives in comfort. This is the prize of everyone who keeps God's law.

4th Person in the crowd
>Perhaps Muhammad is right.

5th Person in the crowd
>Perhaps he is wrong.

6th Person in the crowd
>We don't know that the Angel Gabriel came to Muhammad. He could be making this up.

7th Person in the crowd
>Muhammad has always been against us keeping slaves and worshipping whoever we want. I think we should ignore him.

8th Person in the crowd
>I think we should listen to him.

N And so Muhammad, (pbuh), had a hard time persuading people to follow him. The people of Makkah hated him.

N Only a small group of people were willing to follow Muhammad, (pbuh). They were the first Muslims. Eventually in 622 AD they decided to go off to another town to preach to the people there.

N The people of this town listened to Muhammad, (pbuh) and soon the town was renamed Medina-al-Munawara which means the 'City of the Lights'. Muhammad's leaving Makkah is called the 'hijra'. It means 'departure'. Muslims called this the year one of the Islamic period.

N Muhammad, (pbuh), then spent the rest of his life preaching the word of God.

N The Muslim place of worship is called a mosque and their holy book is called the Qur'an.

N Muslims believe that the Qur'an is the word of God as Gabriel gave it to Muhammad, (pbuh). He recited it to his friends who then wrote it on stones, parchment and leaves or anything on which they could write.

N In 630, eight years after leaving Makkah, he returned to it. By this time his popularity had grown and he became the ruler of Makkah. In 632 AD or 11th year of Islam, Muhammad (pbuh) died.

N Since then, Islam has spread right across the world. Most Muslims live in North Africa and Asia.

N Let us pray.
Oh God, help us always to be brave enough to speak out and say when we know things are wrong. And give us the courage to change things when we can make them better.

Chapter 7 Muslim assemblies

Eid ul-Adha – Celebration of Sacrifice

9th day of the Dhu-al-Hijjah

The festival of Eid ul-Adha is a suitable story for assembly as Ibrahim or Abraham is a revered prophet to Muslims, Jews and Christians. However Jews and Christians believe that it was Isaac, Ibrahim's second son, who was offered as a sacrifice.
It is a movable feast falling on 9th day of the Dhu-al-Hijjah, the 12th month of the Islamic calendar. The dates change each year and are not always the same in each side of the world, because the crescent moon does not always appear on exactly the same date.
The following dates may be useful but can be subject to change.

2007	20th December
2008	8th December
2009	28th November
2010	17th November
2011	7th November

Characters

Ibrahim
Sarah, his wife
Hajar, her maid-servant, later Ibrahim's wife
Ismail, Ibrahim and Hajar's son
Voice from Heaven
Angel
Satan, the devil
Lots of narrators

(*All of the class on stage.*)

N	Good morning and welcome to our assembly. We would like to tell you about the Muslim festival of Eid-Ul-Adha. It is an important Muslim festival which celebrates Ibrahim proving his loyalty to God by showing that he was willing to sacrifice his son Ibrahim.

N	To Muslims, Ibrahim is one of the most important prophets after Muhammad, (pbuh). Ibrahim is also important to both Jews and Christians, who called him Abraham. We would like to tell you his story.

N	In a desert land thousands of years ago,
The heat made it hard for crops to grow.
Back in the cradle of civilization
Life at that time bore no relation
To the life of comfort we have today.

N	There was no technology and no machines No labour-saving gadget had ever been seen. In the Land of Ur in the desert sand Lived a good and loyal God-fearing man.
N	God was pleased with his servant Ibrahim And decided to make a covenant with him And reward him for his loyal behaviour. His place in history was now sure.

(*Ibrahim steps forward and listens to the voice.*)

Voice	Go, Ibrahim, out of this barren land Take as much food and drink as you can. Take Sarah your wife and Lot your nephew. Pack your belongings, your goats and sheep too. I'll take you all to a land that I'll give to you. This is a covenant I am making with you.

(*Ibrahim mimes speaking to Sarah and the servants. They mime packing and gathering their flocks - children on all fours – and going on a journey with Ibrahim and Sarah at the front.*)

N	Ibrahim packed his blankets and his tent, And out of Ur he and Sarah went. They pitched camp at night and travelled by day. They came to Bethel, passing Canaan on the way.

(*Everyone stands and listens to the voice.*)

Voice	This, Ibrahim, is the place where you will stay. This land is your family's for every generation. And I will make you a very great nation. Your descendants will be as many as the stars at night. This land I give you will be a beautiful sight, Flowing with crops and herds and prosperity Your people will live in comfort and be free.
Ibrahim	(*Everyone on their knees*) Thank you Lord for giving to me This land flowing with milk and honey.
N	So Ibrahim built an altar in gratitude To God for his land of drinks and food. And sacrificed a sheep where his altar stood.

(*Mimes building an altar with a servant*)

N	Now they settled happily in this new land. Life was finer than they could ever have planned. They had tents and servants and plenty to eat. They had milk and bread and fruit and meat.

(*They sit in a semicircle facing the audience and mime eating contentedly. Ibrahim turns to look at Sarah affectionately and puts his arm round her.*)

N Now Ibrahim dearly loved his wife Sarah.
He thought no woman could be fairer
In beauty and love, but they had one regret.
Sarah hadn't had any children yet.

(*Everyone exits except Ibrahim and Sarah.*)

N The years went on but no baby was born.
Sarah, disappointed, began to mourn
The loss of motherhood, so she had a ploy
Which she hoped would bring her a baby boy.

Sarah To solve our problem, we don't need to look far.
Marry my hand-maid, the beautiful Hajar.

(*Hajar enters and stands by the side of the stage.*)

I'm far too old now to have a child.
But Hajar is youthful and gentle and mild.
You and she can have a baby for me.
I'm sure it will work. Try it and see.

(*Ibrahim approaches Hajar, speaks to her and they exit together.*)

N And sure enough the plan was a good one.
Eventually Hajar was expecting her son.

(*Hajar re-enters and the two women look at each other in a hostile manner.*)

But bad feeling grew between Sarah and her servant.
Sarah was angry and became fervent
In her wish to get rid of the lovely Hajar.

(*Exit Sarah*)

N Now Hajar was in great distress
And wanted to escape from her mistress.

(*Hajar looks around anxiously and walks around the stage or hall looking for water.*)

She ran away from their comfortable home
And in the desert she had to roam,
Frightened and tired on her own.

N Desperate and in danger of becoming ill.
She went looking for water in the hills.

(*She lies down on the stage where everyone can see her.*)

At last she fell and feared she was dying,
But close by the spot where she was lying
The ground opened and up came a spring
Of cool, fresh water sprinkling the air.
And that was the end of Hajar's despair.

(*Hajar sits up and drinks from the spring.*)

N	She drank until her thirst was gone, Not knowing an angel was looking on.
Angel	Hajar why are you suffering here?
Hajar	Sarah hates me. I was living in fear. I have run away. Have I done wrong?
Angel	Of course, Hajar. No one lives long, Alone in the desert. You must return home. Remember you are carrying the master's son. You will be safe. I know you are loathe To return, but God will take care of you both. Your child will be born a healthy boy. He will give his father love and joy. His name will be Ismail and he will be The head of an enormous family. His children and grandchildren and great-grandchildren too Will spread across this country, through Desert and mountains over land and sea. Across every eastern kingdom and country.

(*Hajar mimes returning home*)

N	So tired and footsore, Hajar returned To the mistress who had recently spurned Her. Soon her son Ismail was born, Amid Ibrahim's love and Sarah's scorn.

(*Enter Ismail with Ibrahim. They sit down and Ibrahim mimes talking to Ismail.*)

N	Now the years went on and Ismail grew. He was healthy and strong and he knew All about his father's devotion to God. He helped his father and loved him well. He loved to listen while his father would tell Him the word of God and his covenant. And Ismail became God's loving servant.

(*They mime building an altar and sacrificing a sheep.*)

N	Now sacrifices to God were still made. A sheep or a goat was carefully laid On a carefully prepared pyre. Ibrahim killed the animal and set it on fire, And Ismail watched and they kneeled in prayer To give thanks to God that their life was fair.
N	Ismail's life was comfortable and carefree. He had loving parents and his life was happy.

(*Exit Ismail*)

	Until one day, like a bolt from the blue God told Ibrahim what to do.
Voice	Make an altar as you have always done Take your son, your only son,

	Put him on the sacrificial altar.
N	Ibrahim was shocked but did not falter. As he listened and heard the worst.
Voice	As a sign that your duty to God comes first Give your son as an offering.
Ibrahim	This will cause me great suffering But I will obey God's command, In gratitude that he has given me this land. How can I now break this news to Ismail? How his mother will weep and wail!
N	Ibrahim sat quietly, devastated. Along came Ismail and he related To him what God had said.

(*Enter Ismail*)

Ibrahim	My son, Father, I don't know how to say this. So far together we've had a life of bliss. But our happy life must now finish. God has asked for the greatest sacrifice I know. I must sacrifice you, my dearest, to show My complete devotion to Him.
Ismail	It's all right Father, God knows best. Your goodness will stand the test. We will go off alone, just you and me, Into the hills and God will see You offer me as a sacrifice We'll meet again in Paradise.

(*Enter Hajar. They say good-bye and walk along together.*)

N	The brave Father and son kissed Hajar good-bye I'm sure each one of them wondered why God was asking such a price: Such an enormous sacrifice.

(*Enter Satan, the devil*)

N	But as they walked along the road, Along came the Devil himself to goad The faithful men from their task.
Satan(*Aside*)	I'll tempt him away from God at last. Hello Ibrahim, good-day Ismail. It's a lovely day, let's go for a sail. There's a pleasant breeze on the lake. Leave your business and let us take A day to relax, for goodness' sake.
Ibrahim	Go away, Satan, we're not interested. You know that you are much detested.
Satan	God doesn't really expect you to kill Your only son. God will still

	Hold you in favour whatever you do.
Ismail	Get lost, Satan, we've had enough of you.
Satan	But what's the rush? Why the hurry? God isn't going to worry Whether it's done today or tomorrow. Grab the day, put off the sorrow.

(*Ibrahim and Ismail lift pieces of sponge wrapped up in brown sugar-paper and throw them at Satan, who flees.*)

Ismail	Get out of here, get on your way You know we'll do what God will say.
N	And so the couple travelled on alone Until they were out of sight of home. They made the altar and piled on the wood Solemnly by the altar Ibrahim stood.

(*Ismail climbs on to the altar and lies down. Ibrahim raises a plastic knife above his head.*)

N	He took out his sharp, short-handled knife And Ismail prepared to give his life. Ismail climbed onto the altar, Determined that he would not falter. Ibrahim watched with tears in his eyes At the thought of this awful sacrifice. And just as the blade was about to fall down They heard the voice of God call down.
Voice	Ibrahim, put away your knife. Your loyalty has saved the life Of your good and loyal son. This sacrifice need not be done. You have both proved your faithfulness. You will both be forever blessed.

(*Ismail jumps down. They hug each other and kneel in a prayer of thanks. Then they mime picking up a sheep, putting it on the altar and sacrificing it.*)

N	Ismail jumped down in delight. Glad that they had both been right To obey God's will, whatever the price So now they made a proper sacrifice. They looked around until they found A sheep lying on the ground. And sacrificed it on the altar mound.
N	In our calendar, the Gregorian calendar, Eid ul-Adha falls on different days. In the Islamic or Muslim calendar, Eid ul-Adha is celebrated on the 10th day of the Month of Dhul Hijja. It comes after Hajj which is the pilgrimage to Makkah, about seventy days after the end of Ramadan. When Muslims go on a Hajj or pilgrimage to the Holy Mosque at Makkah, they remember Ibrahim and Ismail. When they come to the place where Satan, the devil, tempted Ibrahim and Ismail, they throw stones remembering how they drove the devil away.

N   The festival of Eid ul-Adha lasts for three days. On the first day Muslims dress in their best clothes and go to the Mosque to pray. Those who can afford it offer a sacrifice of a sheep, goat, camel or cattle and they are distributed among people who are poor. It is part of the Muslim practice of always looking after people in the community.

N   Let us pray.
Oh God, whatever faith we hold, help us always to keep your laws and behave as you would want us to behave. Help us always to be willing to look after the people around us, not just at religious festivals but all year round.

Alternatively, in a school where there is a Muslim community, you might like to invite a child to say a Muslim prayer.

Chapter 8 Sikh assemblies

Birthday of Guru Gobind Singh

5th January

Guru Gobnd Singh was the tenth and last Sikh Guru. He established the five Ks which are the hallmark of the Sikh population.
If the R.E. resource cupboard contains the five Ks these can be held up at the appropriate time during the performance.

Characters

Guru Gobind Singh
5 Volunteers
Crowd of people
Narrators

(*Start with all the class on the stage, in an arc to step forward to say their part.*)

N	Good afternoon and welcome to our assembly.
N	This week on the 5th January, Sikhs have been celebrating the birthday of Guru Gobind Singh, their 10th Guru. After Guru Nanak, the founder of Sikhism, Guru Gobind Singh is the most important of the ten Sikh Gurus.
N	In India in the 17th century The Sikh population suffered injury. They were persecuted on all sides And attacked by other tribes.
N	Guru Teg Bahadur led his men Against their enemies to defend Their religion and their way of life And to put an end to all the strife.
N	But Teg Bahadur did not survive. He was killed in 1675. His son Gobind was next in line. To be 10th Guru at the age of nine.
N	Though a lad he realized To win they had to be organized. So Guru Gobind took the lead To train a Sikh army and succeed.

N	His army worked in a spirit of unity Fighting only to defend their community. Gobind led his men to victory. And then he planned a life of harmony.
N	He summoned every faithful Sikh To a meeting that was quite unique. In Anandapur they congregated And eagerly the people waited.

(*Gobind stands up in front of the class who are now sitting on the floor listening to him.*)

N	Gobind spoke to the Sikh population.
Gobind	We must be united in determination To stand up for our faith and be ready to fight To defend our religion and our rights. Who is willing to die for their beliefs?
N	At first no one answered. Then to Gobind's relief. A brave man stepped out from the crowd.

1st Volunteer
    I will die for my religion.

N	He was brave and proud.

(*Gobind and volunteer exit*)

N	Then off Gobind and the man went With a flourish into Gobind's tent. In the silence the people heard a swish and a thud. Gobind emerged, his sword covered in blood.

(*Gobind re-enters*)

N	They gasped. Gobind asked the question again.
Gobind	Will anyone else risk being slain?
N	This could not have been anticipated. They were horrified. They were devastated. Another Sikh bravely stepped up from the crowd.

2nd Volunteer (*Stands up*)
    I will die for my religion,

N	he called out loud. Into the tent they disappeared And again just as the people feared, A great swish of a sword echoed over their heads.

Person in the crowd
    Can this be happening to us?

N	they said. Out came Gobind. There was no stopping him. Some swooned in horror that Gobind was chopping limbs From his people. Hadn't they suffered enough From their enemies? Or could this be a bluff?

N	A third stepped up with his head held high.
3rd Volunteer (*Stands up*)	I am not afraid to die.
N	Surely there won't be any more. But up from the crowd stepped number four. And he was followed by number five
5th Volunteer	Dead on earth means in Heaven alive.
N	The people were frantic. They were terrified Imagining what was happening inside That dreaded tent. Could it really be That Gobind could commit an atrocity?
N	They feared their eyes and ears were deceiving them. Were Gobind's senses completely leaving him? The entire crowd was reeling in shock. Their faith in Gobind had taken a knock.

(*The five volunteers re-enter*)

N	The five men emerged from the tent unharmed. There was no need to be alarmed. Guru Gobind looked on his men with great love.
Gobind	These men have shown great faith above All others. From now on they will be Known as the 'Panj piare'. As Sikhs we will preserve our identity We will unite in love and equality. We will form 'Khalsa' which means the 'pure ones' And we'll only admit the faithful and sure ones. And everyone will know us by our ways.'
N	And so Guru Gobind devised the five Ks.

(*If there is a Sikh in the class, he can step forward to display hair and turban.*)

N	Kesh is uncut hair, worn with pride Covered with a turban, hair is tucked inside. Hair must be clean and groomed twice a day And kept in an orderly, tidy way.
N	(*Holding up a kangha*) With a kangha a small comb fixed in place. And worn with dignity and grace.
N	(*Holding up a kara*) A kara, a steel bangle on the right arm Broad at that time to protect from harm.
N	(*Holding up a kirpan*) A kirpan, a knife, a symbol that they will fight Against evil, but only to defend their rights.
N	(*Holding up white shorts*) Kashera, loose shorts, to move easily In white, a sign of purity.

And so Sikhism did survive
Throughout the world, Sikh people thrive.

N	Guru Gobind was the 10th and last human Guru. He said that after his death their holy book would be their only Guru. From that time onwards the holy book became known as the Guru Granth Sahib.

N	He also said that all men should add the name of Singh to their own. It means 'a lion'. He also said that women should take the name of 'Kaur' which means a 'princess.'

(*If you have Sikh children in the class they may be able to perform a song or dance of their own culture.*)

N	Let us pray.
Oh God, help us always to stand for what we believe is right, but never to go looking for a fight. Make us tolerant of each other and willing to treat all people of all races and religions with respect.

Chapter 8 Sikhism

Birthday of Guru Nanak

April

Guru Nanak was the founder of Sikhism and the first Sikh Guru. Although Guru Nanak was born in April 1469, his birthday is celebrated on the full moon of the lunar month of Kartik and so is different each year. This script is made up with short, snappy scenes so each child except Nanak can have two or thee parts.

Characters

Guru Nanak
Nanak's father
Shopkeeper (non-speaking part)
Poor person (non-speaking part)
Nanak's wife
Duni Chand
Duni Chand's servant
Duni Chand's wife
3 Priests
Mardana, a friend of Guru Nanak
2 rich men
Bhai Lalo
Malik Bhago
Malik Bhago's servant
Narrators

(The children can stand at the back or the sides of the stage and go on, when needed, to play their part.)

N	Welcome to our assembly. This week, Sikhs in Britain are celebrating the birthday of Guru Nanak the founder of Sikhism. Every year, Sikhs celebrate his birthday with an important festival called Gurupurab. They go to the Gurdwara for a service and listen to a reading from the Guru Granth Sahib, the Sikh Holy Book. They also have a procession in the street with the Guru Granth Sahib carried on a beautifully decorated throne. We would like to tell you the story of how Sikhism started.

N	In India in 1469,
	In the Punjab's hot, dry clime,
	In Talwindi, west of Lahore,
	A lively boy called Nanak was born.

N	Nanak was a bright and healthy child,
	With a kindly nature, gentle and mild.
	He learnt local languages, Arabic and Persian.
	As a boy, he had a great aversion

	To cruelty or unfair play. His father came to him one day,
Father	You're twelve now Nanak. I want you to Learn about business. Here's some rupees for you. Use them to see what you can do To make the money grow. Buy and sell so you can show A little profit if you can. I want you to be a business man.
N	But profit wasn't Nanak's thing. He was a kindly lad, gentle and caring. He went off to the local shops, Happily in skips and hops. He bought some food and took it to The village poor.

(*Guru skips to a shop and buys some food and carries it to a poor person.*)

Nanak	Here's some food for you.
N	Thinking he'd used the money well. He went off to find his dad to tell.

(*Nanak returns to his father*)

N	Dad, I spent your money on food. I gave it to the poor. Isn't that a good Use of it?
Father	I don't think so. Money is for business to make it grow.
Nanak	Dad, I think I used it for true business. Your money is well-used, I could do no less Than use it for God's work – feeding the poor.

(*Father exits in disgust*)

N	Now this might seem right to me and you But Nanak's family were Hindu. There was a caste system firmly in place. It spoiled the lives of many of the race.
N	They lived in castes, high and low, The high to the low did not show Care or respect. They called them 'untouchable'. To escape from your caste was impossible. Nanak hated the unjust ways That people had in those days.
N	The years passed on and Nanak grew. At sixteen he was given a job to do. He worked in the office of a large store Of the Muslim ruler of Sultanpur.
N	He had a head for figures and was a studious man. He read Hindu scriptures and those of Islam. Now Nanak had a comfortable life.

At eighteen years he took a wife.

(*Wife enters and walks up to Nanak and they link arms.*)

N In their cosy home they lived happily.
And were blessed with two sons in their family.
Nanak was a deeply religious man

Nanak I love to read scriptures when I can.

N He often read late into the night,
Eager to know what God said was right.

(*Nanak mimes swimming and exits*)

One day he went down to the river to swim.
Hours later there was no sign of him.
Everyone searched all around.

Wife I fear my Nanak has been drowned.

N The family were all plunged into grief.
Then a miracle, to everyone's relief.

(*Nanak enters*)

Nanak I've been talking to God these three days.
He has shown me how we must change our ways.
With God there's no Muslim or Hindu.
It is how we live that shows the true
Meaning of religion in our lives.
We are all equal in God's eyes.
With God there is no race or caste.
Let us change this awful system at last.

(*During the next four verses, Nanak and Mardana mime the actions.*)

N Then as Guru Nanak he was known.
The faithful Nanak left his home
On four great journeys he was to roam.
Down through India to the southern coast
Each place they went they made the most
Of every opportunity
To preach God's word to the community.

N Mardana, his trusted Muslim friend
Accompanied Guru Nanak to lend
A hand in his life's mission
To challenge the ancient caste tradition.

N Off to the North the couple set.
Past Afghanistan, and home through Tibet.
People were delighted to see them come.
Many listeners took them home
To eat and give them beds to rest.
They were proud to have these honoured guests.

N Through Iran and Iraq was their quest,
All the way to Arabia in the west.

        And East towards China the travellers walked
        And at each town they preached and talked.

(*Class gathers round to listen.*)

        To spread God's word to the gathered crowd.
        The word of God he preached out loud.

N   To the east they made an expedition
      Spreading the word was their mission.
      For twenty years Guru Nanak was fired
      With missionary zeal until he retired.

N   In Kartapur he settled down.
      Each night people gathered round
      To hear Guru Nanak narrate
      The word of God and meditate.

N   A young man called Lehna joined the group.
      Nanak announced him the next Guru.
      He renamed him Angad which means 'a part of me'.
      Their religion grew in popularity.
      At the age of seventy, Nanak passed away.
      But his words and teachings live on today.

N   Guru Nanak was a very wise man and an excellent teacher. There are many stories about how Guru Nanak taught people to keep God's law. We would like to tell you some of them.

N   This story is called 'The Rich Man and the Needle.' One day Guru Nanak and Mardana were travelling in India, teaching people God's law and how He wanted them to live. One day he arrived in the city of Lahore.

N   People were delighted that he had come to their city, especially Duni Chand, a very wealthy banker. He was eager to meet Guru Nanak.

(*Enter Duni Chand to meet Guru Nanak.*)

Duni Chand   Guru Nanak, I am having a banquet tomorrow night. I would love you to come and be my guest of honour.

Guru Nanak   Thank you, but no thank you. Really I just like a plain meal. Anyway you might not like my company.

Duni Chand   Nonsense, that could never happen. Please come to my house. The food will be delicious. The best you have ever eaten.

Guru Nanak   All right, I shall come.

Duni Chand   Wonderful. I am delighted.

N   Duni Chand went home to make sure everything was properly prepared for his important guest.

(*Exit Guru Nanak. Enter Duni Chand's servant.*)

Duni Chand   Make sure everything is perfect. I want Guru Nanak to be treated with great care.

Servant   Yes, Duni Chand. We will make sure everything is just as you want it.

N   The next evening the guests arrived and everyone took up their seats.

(Half of the class enter and shake hands with Duni Chand and sit in a semicircle. Duni Chand sits in the middle with Guru Nanak beside him. Some children serve the food and they eat and chatter among themselves. Comments about the fine food can be heard above the conversation.)

Duni Chand   I hope you have enjoyed your meal, Guru Nanak.

Guru Nanak   Yes, thank you.

Duni Chand   Guru Nanak, I am a very rich man. I can give you anything that money can buy. Tell me anything that I can give you and you shall have it.

(Guru Nanak thinks quietly for a few seconds. He takes a small box out of his pocket and takes a needle out of it.)

Guru Nanak   Yes, Duni Chand, here is a job I should like you to do for me. Take this needle and look after it for me. When we meet in Heaven give it back to me.

Duni Chand (*Thrilled*)
       Yes Guru Nanak. I shall take good care of it and you shall have it back in Heaven.

N   The evening passed pleasantly and the guests went home.

(Guests stand up and shake hands with Duni Chand and Guru Nanak and everyone leaves.)

Duni Chand   Look, my dear. Guru Nanak has given me a special task. He wants me to look after this needle for him and give it back to him in Heaven.

Wife   (*Laughing*) And how can you do that? How can you possibly take a needle to the next world with you when you die? I think you had better ask him how he expects you to carry something from one world to the next.

(Exit wife)

N   The next day, Duni Chand went to find Guru Nanak.

(Enter Guru Nanak)

Duni Chand   Guru Nanak, how can I take this needle into the next world with me.

Guru Nanak   What is the difficulty? The needle is so tiny and light. If you cannot take a tiny, little thing like that into the next world, how can you take all your money and belongings with you?

Duni Chand   I see what you mean. All my money and belongings are useless to me in the next world since I can't take them with me to Heaven when I die. I should give more of my belongings away, since I cannot use them all anyway.

(He exits)

N   So Duni Chand changed his way of living. He gave money and food away to the poor and always tried to help anyone in trouble. When he died he took a lot of love to Heaven with him.

N   In this story, Guru Nanak taught the man that generosity was more valuable than money.

N   The next story about Guru Nanak is called 'The Milk and the Jasmine Flower.'

N   Guru Nanak spent twenty years travelling and teaching in India and the countries

	around it. His Muslim friend, Mardana the musician, accompanied him on lots of his journeys.
N	One day they decided to go to the city of Multan. It was a city which had lots of priests. People in India travelled a long way to go the city of Multan for advice from the priests. Then they gave the priests expensive gifts for their advice and so the priests became rich.
1st Priest	Have you heard that Guru Nanak and Mardana are coming to Multan?
2nd Priest	If he comes, he will talk to the people and give them advice for a bowl of rice.
3rd Priest	People will not want to listen to us if Guru Nanak is here.
1st Priest	How can we stop him coming?
2nd Priest	I know how to stop him coming. Let us fill a bowl to the brim with milk. I shall ask my servant to take it to Guru Nanak and tell him the city is full like this bowl and there is no room for another priest.
3rd Priest	Great idea. Perhaps he will go away.

(*Exit priests*)

N	And so the servant was sent to meet Guru Nanak and his friend Mardana.
Mardana	This has been a long walk and I am so hungry and thirsty. I hope we can soon rest in Multan.

(*Enter servant carrying a bowl with white sugar paper on top*)

Servant	Guru Nanak, my master has asked me to tell you that the city of Multan is full like this bowl of milk which they have asked me to give to you. There is no more room for even one more person.
Mardana	That milk looks lovely, Guru Nanak, and I'm so thirsty.

(*Guru Nanak picks a jasmine flower made of sugar paper and drops it into the bowl of milk.*)

Guru Nanak	See how the Jasmine flower floats on top without the milk spilling. Tell your master that no matter how full a place is, there is always room for more goodness and holiness.

(*Exit Guru Nanak and Mardana. Priests enter*)

Servant	Guru Nanak sent the bowl back with the jasmine flower on top. He says that there is always more room for wisdom.
2nd Priest	I am ashamed. We have been so nasty and unfriendly.
N	The three priests went off to find Guru Nanak.

(*Nanak, Mardana and the priests enter.*)

2nd Priest	I am so sorry. We should have made you welcome.
1st Priest	Please come and stay in our town.
3rd Priest	Please come and stay at my house and have supper with me.

(*They exit*)

N	Guru Nanak and Mardana stayed in the town and preached to the townspeople. In

this story, Guru Nanak reminded the priests that in God's eyes, everyone is of the same value and that the world is big enough for each one of us.

N On another of Guru Nanak's travels he and Mardana went to the town of Aimanabad. When they arrived lots of people wanted them to stay at their houses.

(*Enter Guru Nanak, Mardana and two rich men*)

1st Rich man
Stay with me, Guru Nanak. I have a large house and you will be very comfortable.

2nd Rich man
Come to my house Guru Nanak. We have lots of food in. You will have plenty to eat.

Guru Nanak Thank you but I have already accepted an invitation to stay with Bhai Lalo in his home behind his carpentry shop.

(*Exit Guru Nanak and Mardana*)

1st Rich man
Why does he want to stay with Bhai Lalo. Doesn't he know that he is a poor carpenter and he would be much more comfortable in one of our homes.

2nd Rich man
He will be sorry when he sees his home.

(*Exit the rich men. Enter Bhai Lalo.*)

N Guru Nanak and Mardana stayed at Bhai Lalo's house for some days.

Bhai Lalo I hope you have enough to eat. The food here is very plain.

Mardana The food is fine Bhai Lalo.

Guru Nanak Your food is served with kindness. We are enjoying our stay here.

(*Knock at the door*)

Bhai Lalo I'll find out who is at the door. (*He mimes opening the door.*)

Servant My master has asked me to deliver this invitation to Guru Nanak and Mardana.

Mardana (*Reading*)
Malik Bhago would like the company of Guru Nanak and Mardana at a feast at his home tomorrow night.

Guru Nanak I do not want to go. Say to your master, thank you but no thank you.

(*Exit Nanak, Mardana and Bhai Lalo. Enter Malik Bhago.*)

N The servant returned to his master, Malik Bhago.

Servant I have delivered the invitation but Guru Nanak said, 'Thank you, but no thank you'.

Malik Bhago I am very disappointed. I was looking forward to having Guru Nanak in my home. I want to talk to him.

(*Exit servant. Enter Guru Nanak and Mardana.*)

N Next day, Malik Bhago saw Guru Nanak walking by his home and he called him into his home.

Malik Bhago Guru Nanak. I am angry that you would not eat in my home. You stay at the home of Bhai Lalo, a poor man and yet you will not eat in my home. I am very upset that you prefer a poor man's food to mine.

Guru Nanak Let me show you why.

(*He mimes*)

Here is some bread from your home and here is some bread for Bhai Lalo's home. Look at what happens when we squeeze them both.

Mardana From the coarse bread of Bhai Lalo's home comes milk and from the fine bread from your home comes blood. Your bread is earned from treating the people who work for you harshly, and not paying them a fair wage. Bhai Lalo's bread is earned by honest, hard work and dealing with his customers fairly and kindly.

Guru Nanak Now you know why we prefer to eat at Bhai Lalo's home.

N And so Guru Nanak taught the man that honesty and kindness made much better company than riches.

N Let us pray.
Oh God, Thank you for the lessons that Guru Nanak taught because they are suitable for people of every religion. Help us always to be honest and to deal fairly with every person in every race and religion.

Chapter 9 Secular assemblies

Rahere the Jester

d. 1144

Jesters from history were colourful characters, loved by their masters and under-rated by others. Rahere, the jester to Henry 1st has been immortalised by his legacy to the nation. His story is told today in the stained glass windows which decorate the walls of the Priory Church of St Bartholomew's Hospital in Smithfield in the City of London.

> **Characters**
>
> Rahere
> King Henry 1st
> People at court
> Inn-keeper
> Inn-keeper's wife
> St Bartholomew
> People ill
> Lots of narrators

(A scene at the king's court. People are standing round, chatting to each other, hoping to get the chance to talk to the king, who is distinguishable from the others by his crown. Rahere the jester is close at hand, ready to attend to the king, if needed.)

N In days of old, when knights were bold,
And videos weren't invented,
Each time the king, felt like a sing
His jester then presented
A song and a dance and story or two
And kept the king contented.

N They were often friends, the king and his fool.
They laughed and joked, they were really cool.
They shared their secrets, helped each other along,
Relaxed in the evening with their lutes and a song.

(King approaches Rahere and puts his arm around his shoulder.)

N Henry the First loved his jester dear.
A talented clown was the brave Rahere.
With a snazzy suit of black and red,
When Henry was sad, Rahere sped
With a coxcombe stuck on the end of his staff,
He joked and fooled and made Henry laugh.

King Tell me a joke Rahere.

(Children love jokes. They can probably add alist to the ones below.)

Rahere Why are tall people lazy?

King I don't know. Why are tall people lazy?

Rahere Because they lie longest in bed.

(The courtiers all look at the king to see if he laughs. Only when he starts to laugh do the rest of them laugh.)

Rahere What did the doctor say to the man who kept saying he was a pair of curtains?

King I don't know. What did he say?

Rahere Oh, pull yourself together!

(Everyone laughs)

King I'm in the mood for singing. Let's have a song.

(The class can sing any song which they enjoy at the time. It doesn't have to be Medieval. It is also an opportunity for a child to play an instrument. Exit all.)

N But tragedy struck, enormous woe!
Happiness ended, Rahere had to go.
Henry's brave son was in the Channel one day.
A dreadful storm blew his ship away.

(Use a sail made out of two metre sticks joined at right angles and a piece of white sugar paper hanging from the cross-bar. A few children holding the 'mast and sail' rush from side to side across the stage to symbolize the ship in difficulty and eventually sinking.)

N 'Neath the ocean wave everyone drowned.
When the White Ship hit the sandy ground.
And all the crew were sadly mourned.

(Enter Rahere and king)

Henry the First was miserable, forlorn.
He told his Rahere,

Henry I shall never again.
Dance or sing a happy refrain
I've finished with stories and knights
And banquets and parties and brave sword fights.
I shall mourn every day for the loss of my son.
(Or marry again and get another one.)
But in the meantime you must leave here.
Take a holiday, my good Rahere.

(Rahere sets off walking round the hall and back to the stage.)

Rahere I'll go to Rome and see the pope,
Until the king learns to cope.
I'll pack my bags and walk to Dover
To the good old Channel and I'll cross over.
I'll walk through France, cadging meals and lifts,
I'll go on a pilgrimage bearing gifts,

	For the church of Rome, in the hope that God
	Will find a way to get me back my job.
N	One day he approached a little French town.
	A nasty disease struck him down.

(Enter inn-keeper and wife who feed him and put him to bed.)

N	The inn-keeper made sure he was fed
	And the landlady put him straight to bed.
N	He was homesick now and began to weep
	Before sinking into a deep, deep sleep.
	He dreamed of home, the Tower and the king,
	St Bartholomew then appeared to him.

(Enter people in Rahere's dream – St Bartholomew, people crippled, ill.)

St Bartholomew
    Look at those people, they're limp and crying.
    Crippled, diseased and ill and dying.
    Go back to England's pleasant land
    And ask the king for a bit of ground.
    Build a hospital to care for the sick.
    There's no time to lose. Hurry, quick!

(Exit Bartholomew and people.)

N	Rahere awoke from this heartening dream.
	He was fired up with this new scheme.
	His infection fled. With determination
	To put his plan into operation
	He journeyed north up through France.
N	His heart was longing for a song and a dance.
	This great new plan had given him zest
	To reach his home without a rest.
	He was desperate to start his new job in life.
	Luckily the king had found a new wife.
N	He went to the king as soon as he arrived.
Rahere	Your majesty, I was ill but I survived.
	I thought I was lying in my death bed,
	But St Bartholomew visited me and said,
	'Get off that bed and go back home.
	There's a lot of valuable work to be done.'
	Your majesty, please can you provide
	Land for a hospital? Too many have died
	Of nasty illnesses and diseases.
N	King Henry swiftly gave him leases
	Of some smooth but marshy land
	For the great new hospital he'd planned
	To relieve the Londoners of plague
	And illnesses, handicap and ague.
N	So if one day you happen to be
	In the City of London, you can see

St Bartholomew's Hospital and the Priory
Church. Its stained glass windows show a clear
Story in pictures of the jester Rahere.

N   Let us pray.
Oh God, Thank you for the life of Rahere and his hard work in building St Bartholomew's hospital, which has done such wonderful health work for Britain for nine hundred years.

Chapter 9 Secular assemblies

Blondel the Jester

mid 12th century

This is a terrific story for demonstrating love and loyalty of a good friend. It is also a super opportunity to have fun.
As in the story of Rahere the king wears a crown made out of a piece of card, or one out of a Christmas cracker would do. For a musical instrument a recorder would be good enough.
For the speeches with jokes in the king and jester's conversation, you can use the ones below or ask your class to suggest some. They will appreciate being involved in scripting the performance. It does not matter if they are not Medieval, as long as the children speak up well and are enjoying themselves. Similarly, the song they use does not have to be Medieval. If they sing something they enjoy they will sing up well and that is much more important.

> **Characters**
>
> King Richard
> Blondel
> A messenger
> People at court (non-speaking part)
> Soldiers (non-speaking part)
> Lots of narrators

(A court scene. The class stand around, in groups, chatting and looking occasionally at the king.)

N Good morning and welcome to our assembly. We are going to tell you the story of a great, unsung hero. Blondel the jester was a marvellous example of a brave and devoted friend to Richard I, the Lionheart King.

N Richard the first was the Lionheart King.
A jolly young monarch who loved to sing.
A talented musician, he played on his flute
And made up tunes on his harp and lute.

(King Richard strides across the stage to Blondel, wearing a crown and carrying a musical instrument.)

N His closest friend was his jester, Blondel.
To him his troubles he would tell.

(Blondel walks over to the king smiling affectionately and the king puts his arm around his shoulders and they mime a conversation.)

N King and jester sang together
Rode and hunted in all kinds of weather.

King Cheer me up, Blondel. Tell me a joke.

Blondel	Why did the skeleton not go to the ball?
King	I don't know. Why not?
Blondel	Because he had no body to go with him.

(*Laughter from the rest of the class*)

Blondel	Why did the boy eat his homework?
King	I don't know. Why did he eat his homework?
Blondel	Because his teacher said it was a piece of cake.

(*More laughter*)

King	Let's have a song.

(*The whole class gathers round and sings whatever the class happens to be learning in their music lessons at the time. Alternatively, this could be replaced with any English folk dance.*)

N	But Richard was a restless ruler. Really he thought it would be cooler To stride abroad in foreign wars. Any old excuse – a religious cause.
Blondel	Why aren't you content to stay At home with me to hunt and play?
Richard	Because I want to go down in history As a king of adventure and bravery.

(*King strides across the stage, restlessly flexing his muscles and brandishing a plastic sword.*)

> The English don't remember minstrels.
> They love great heroes, strong and invincible.
> I want to be a warrior, not just to play.
> I want to attack and fight and slay.

(*Swishes sword around looking vicious*)

N	So off he went, sword in hand To fight the Saracens in a foreign land.

(*King strides off-stage followed by a few pairs of soldiers.*)

N (*Aside*)	Silly old Richard didn't know, Muslims worship the same God you know.

(*Exit Blondel*)

N	But after years of fierce crusading, Richard's battle strength was fading.

(*Enter king looking dishevelled and fainting. Two Saracens grab him, one under each armpit and lead him off the stage.*)

N	At last it happened, his might was tested. The battle lost, he was arrested And thrown into a nasty jail.

N	He sat there miserably growing pale. Back to England a messenger raced.

(Enter messenger)

Messenger	Our king is captured. We are disgraced. I'm afraid they'll ask for a king's ransom. For poor old Richard, so brave and handsome.

(Blondel puts his head in his hands and weeps.)

N	Blondel heard the news and wept. Onto his trusty horse he leapt. His lute was packed in seconds flat With his purse and cloak and warmest hat.

(Blondel mimes packing and riding off.)

N	Off to the coast Blondel sped Praying that Richard wasn't dead. To each French castle he did ride And jumped off his horse and sang outside.

(Blondel mimes singing)

N	He played and sang all Richard's songs. His journeys were cold and tiring and long. With sinking heart he tried every day. Beside each castle he would sing and play.

(Blondel continues miming riding, looking tired and singing.)

N	For months brave Blondel sought his king. One day by a castle he stopped to sing. He sang for an hour by the castle's west. He was sad and tired and stopped for a rest.

(Enter king at the other side of the stage.)

N	What do you think in his ears was ringing?
N	The joyous sound of King Richard singing.

(Both mime singing, or they might actually sing a verse aloud if they can do a duet.)

	Together they sang and sang with delight. Soon King Richard would be back in the fight!
N	Then began a frenzy of activity To save King Richard from captivity. At last the ransom was agreed And Richard the Lionheart was freed.
N	Back to his friends and countrymen Richard returned, overjoyed, and then They celebrated, ate and drank well

To the health and loyalty of brave Blondel.

(Everyone cheers)

N Let us pray.
Please God help us to be loyal friends, who are always ready to help others when they are in trouble.

Chapter 9 King Alfred the Great

King Alfred the Great

849 – 899

King Alfred, the Saxon king of Wessex, is the only king in our history who has been awarded the title of 'the Great'. After making peace with the Vikings and dividing England between them, he took his part of the country out of the Dark Ages into a new era by setting up schools, churches and building up an army and navy. Sir Winston Churchill called him the greatest Englishman who ever lived.
His story is also covered on the history topic of Invaders and Settlers so this script can be used to re-inforce your class work. This script is made up of short, snappy scenes.

Characters

King Alfred
Briton
2 Saxons
Wessex soldiers   (Most of these double up as his council at the end.)
Dane soldiers
Peasant woman
Guthrum
2 Saxon thanes
Lots of narrators

(The class can stand at the back of the stage or in the wings ready to step forward to play their parts.)

N	Good morning and welcome to our assembly. Our form would like to tell you about King Alfred the Great.
N	Why Great?
N	King Alfred is the only king in the whole history of the United Kingdom to be given the title of Great after his name. Many people say he did more for Britain than any other monarch. Winston Churchill called him the greatest Englishman ever.
N	What did he do?
N	He saved Britain from being totally taken over by the Vikings and he then went on to turn his half of the kingdom into a much safer place. He built up an army and the first navy.
N	He was a Christian who had lots of churches built and he believed that people should be able to read and write so he started up schools. Winchester School was founded by King Alfred. He took Britain out of the Dark Ages and modernized it. Let us go back to 867 to tell you the story from the beginning.
N	Way, way back, eleven centuries ago. The standard of living was rather low. There was no electricity, phones or cars.

	Life for the Brits was fairly harsh.
N	The Saxons had been here for many generations. They didn't read or write and had no education. No writing down means no information. So we don't know much of this illiterate nation.
N	That is why it is called the Dark Ages. The Saxons were suffering the battle rages Of the Vikings attacking them in the east Stealing all of value and each farmyard beast.

(Enter a Briton and two Saxons)

Briton	My family have lived in Eboracum for generations. They came over with the Romans because one of my ancestors was in the army. He liked it and brought the whole family, so they settled down and stayed even after the Roman army went back to defend Rome.
1st Saxon	My family came from Denmark. They were farmers. Their land was getting flooded at times and it was becoming more difficult to grow enough crops to feed the family. They heard the Romans had left Britain and the land was covered with forests so there was plenty of wood to build houses and the forests had lots of deer and wild hog.
2nd Saxon	Mine came from Germany. They heard the land was great for growing crops and so they packed up and came here.
Briton	Our families have been living here for centuries. It's terrible that we now have to suffer these awful attacks from the Vikings.
1st Saxon	Where do they come from?
2nd Saxon	They come from Norway, Sweden and Denmark. They are the best sailors in the world and they have become wealthy by trading with people all over Europe. They've even been to that icy land in the far north-west. Iceland or something they call it.
Briton	My grandmother lived on the east coast. She says that the Vikings arrived one day and attacked their local abbey. They killed the monks and stole all the gold plates and ate all their food. They even burnt their books. And now they are attacking us. They've taken over Eboracum and given it a new name, they call it Jorvik.
1st Saxon	They've taken over Northumbria and Mercia and got rid of their kings. And now they're going to attack Wessex. I wonder how King Aethelwulf will like that.
2nd Saxon	They'll probably drive him out like the others.
Briton	Just wait and see. He's a fierce man and he's got strong sons. I think he'll give them a hard time before he gives up.

(During the next four verses the Dane soldiers and Saxon soldiers pair up and mime fighting. They must not actually touch each other. At the last line, they are all exhausted.)

N	And so the population waited And watched what happened with bated Breath. Aethelwulf died, Aethelred was next. The Vikings made him sorely vexed When they attacked in 870. But the Wessex men defended their territory.

N	One year later the war was rife. They all prepared for the strife. Soon the armies met near Ashdown On a hill with the Vikings fighting down.
N	But the Wessex army fought with skill And slashed and chopped their way uphill, Defeated the Vikings and won the day But the Viking army wasn't going away.
N	The next year with battles was filled. The Saxons were defeated and Aethelred killed. Young Alfred became king at twenty-one And a vicious war was begun.

(Exit soldiers in the background, except three Wessex soldiers.)

1st Wessex soldier
>Those Vikings are a vicious lot. They're crafty too. Did you see how they managed to get to the top of the hill to fight us at Ashdown?

2nd Wessex soldier
>We beat them anyway. Did you see how that young Prince Alfred fought that Dane? He was much bigger than Alfred but the young prince was far too quick for him.

3rd Wessex soldier
>Shame we couldn't keep it up. At those other battles the Danes were too strong for us.

1st Wessex soldier
>Looks like they've beaten us now. They've taken over a large chunk of Wessex. I couldn't believe it when they took over the town of Cheltenham. They're safe in there.

2nd Wessex soldier
>They've destroyed a lot of Wessex. They've killed thousands of people and thousands have had to run away and hide. Lots of them have gone to the Isle of Wight for safety.

3rd Wessex soldier
>I don't know what's happened to young King Alfred.

1st Wessex soldier
>Some say he's gone off to hide in the marshlands in Somerset. He's got a small bunch of thanes with him and they're waiting for their chance to fight back at the end of the winter.

2nd Wessex soldier
>Some chance of that. I think we're condemned to a life time of Dane rule.

N	By now Alfred was on the run. His most dangerous days had begun. One day, so the legend says, Alfred was having the worst of days.
N	He was trying to escape from some Danes And drenched right through by the wind and rain. Breathless he ran helter-skelter, Saw a cottage and asked for shelter.

(Alfred knocks and a peasant woman appears)

Woman	What do you want?
Alfred	I'm a poor farmer, searching for a sheep I've lost on the hills. Can you allow me a little shelter until the rain stops and I dry out.
Woman	Don't touch anything in my home. I'm going out to feed the hens and lock them in for the night. Sit there by the fire and watch my cakes. When you can smell that they're done, lift them out.
Alfred	Thank you. You're a kind woman. I'll look after them.

(She goes out)

N	Wearily Alfred looked about. He took off his coat to dry it out. He looked out of the window anxiously Searching for signs of the enemy.
N	He couldn't see the Danes anywhere So he went to the fire and took a chair. Poor old Alfred. Exhausted he slept. The cakes burned. His word wasn't kept.

(Woman re-enters, shouts and hits Alfred who runs away.)

N	Now Alfred was a resourceful man He sat down with his friends to plan A way to get themselves out of this jam.
N	They built a fortress in Somerset Its strong and sturdy structure let The Wessex army be secure While they practised for the war.
N	The armies met at Edington. The Saxons attacked with fury and won. They pursued them back to their Viking fortress Defeated and hungry in great distress.
N	So, to Alfred's great relief, The Danes gave in and begged for peace. The two kings met in the town of Wedmore. To discuss a way to end the war.

(Enter Guthrum, Alfred, and a few companions of each.)

Guthrum	My people would like peace. We want to end the war.
Alfred	I am willing to stop fighting but we must be absolutely certain that the Danes will never attack any part of Wessex ever again.
Guthrum	I agree to that.
Alfred	And you must become a Christian.
Guthrum	But...
Alfred	No buts! If you want to avoid being hammered by the Wessex Saxons again, you must have it on my terms. You will become a Christian and I shall be your Godfather.

Guthrum	All right. I agree. But what about land? My people have already settled themselves in the North and East of Angleland.
Alfred	Just make sure all of your fighters go back to their own part of the country and as long as they stay away from Wessex, we will not attack them.
N	They lived in peace until 886 And the two kings met again to fix Terms for a permanent agreement Of a land settlement.

(Alfred and Guthrum sit down together and study map.)

N	They sat down together and planned How to divide up the land. Both kings were fairly pleased To draw a line north-west south-east From Chester to London about Watling Street Would be the border where the two lands meet.
N	Danelaw in the north and west Would with Viking law be blest. And Alfred could only be pleased For he gained land in the south and east.

(They shake hands and exit.)

N	And so the two men went back To their home and no more attacked Each other. Now Alfred planned his reign. Determined to make Wessex strong again.
N	A clever, practical man he knew Exactly what he needed to do. He knew their success was in relation To defence and trade and education. A sincere and religious man He restored religion in his land.
Alfred	*(Addressing his council)* We will make absolutely certain, our realm is safe from ever being invaded again. We will build fortresses across the land to defend ourselves. We will have a fyrd system. Half of the thanes in the land will come together with half of their churls for six months of the year and they will be our trained army. The half who stay at home will do the farming for their village. Every six months they will swap places with the other half of the country's thanes and churls so we will always have an army ready and plenty of food for everyone.
1st Thane	We can still be attacked by sea. The Jutes in the north can still sail down to the Channel and attack us in the south.
2nd Thane	We must build ships and train a naval force to defend our coastline.
Alfred	Religion has begun to die out since the Vikings destroyed our abbeys. I want churches built and monasteries restored. We need education in our land. I will build schools to educate the sons of thanes.
N	Alfred did all of this for his country. He kept it safe and modernized it, lifting it out of the Dark Ages.

N   That's why he is called Alfred the Great.

N   Let us pray.
Oh God, we know we cannot all be great men and women, but help us all to remember that it is always important to work hard and do everything as well as we can.

Chapter 9   Secular assemblies

William Shakespeare

1564 – 1616, 23rd April

This is an alternative script for St George's day, which is generally accepted as being William Shakespeare's birthday and co-incidentally the day of his death.
Increasingly, teachers are being encouraged to make ICT an integral part of their lessons. This script, which is completely narrative, can be illustrated with an attractive PowerPoint program using pictures from the Internet. Pupils could find the pictures which best illustrate the verses which they recite. If pupils key

www.google.co.uk 'the life of William Shakespeare' and 'the plays of William Shakespeare' and

www.yahoo.com 'the 37 plays of William Shakespeare,' there will be a vast number of images from which to choose.

(Everyone on stage to recite their parts in turn.)

N	Good morning and welcome to our assembly. This week on 23rd April, it will not only be St George's day, but also the day which is likely to be the birthday of England's finest playwright, William Shakespeare. Our class would like to entertain you with our PowerPoint program about the story of his life and work.
N	In England in the 16th Century There ruled the Tudor Dynasty. And merry England was the place to be.
N	The Wars of the Roses had come and gone. The battles lost and battles won. And good Queen Bess sat on the throne.
N	In the Warwickshire town of Stratford-on-Avon, In the heart of England's pleasant haven Of forests and rivers, in 1564 For her husband John, Mary Shakespeare bore An infant son on St George's day. His name was William, by the way.
N	In the local church he was baptized. No one could have realized That William Shakespeare was a special child With imagination, romantic and wild. Drama and poetry would roll off his tongue, His songs and poems forever sung.
N	Drama was popular in those days. Travelling theatres performed their plays.

William Shakespeare loved to see
A performing drama company.

N   Inspired by shows and his love of rhyme
William Shakespeare passed his time
Watching plays and reading history.
He was passionate about the mystery
Of poetry and drama and songs and dance
Tragedy, comedy and romance.

N   In the Stratford town he must have been
An avid pupil – a schoolmaster's dream.
In school holidays William explored
The woods around the town of Stratford.
By trees and herbs he passed his days.
We know, for he mentioned them in his plays.

N   Our William married young in life.
At eighteen years he took a wife
His bride was Anne Hathaway.
Unfortunately he did not stay.

N   Cities beckoned men of skill,
And off to London went our Will.
London was a noisy, bustling place.
Dusty and smoky with everyone's waste
Thrown on the street, a filthy place.

N   The most exciting city in the land.
With ale-houses, bear-pits, beggars and
Thieves to pinch the cash from your pocket.
When you jostled in busy crowds in the market.

N   There was only one thing in his head.
Towards the theatre his ambition led.
William had a theatrical bent.
To the theatre in Curtain Road he went.

N   Several happy years he spent
As an apprentice learning the trade.
William worked hard and made the grade.
An actor's life was real hard graft.
To learn each detail of the craft.

N   Singing and dancing and acrobatics
Were par for the course of theatrics.
He learnt the art of dramatized fighting
But William's talent lay in writing.

N   The theatre owners realized soon
An in-house writer is such a boon.
William's pen worked overtime
In drama, sonnets, songs and rhyme.

N   He remembered his history lessons in school.
Converting them to plays was really cool.
We know that by 1592,
Shakespeare's plays had made their breakthrough.

N   His three plays of Henry VI's reign
Were performed over and over again.

| | He remembered the classics lessons he'd sat in.
He recalled the stories he'd read in Latin.
And churned them out in his comedies.
And made people weep with his tragedies. |
|---|---|
| N | Queen Elizabeth herself was enthralled,
And so William was sometimes called
To entertain the nation's queen.
Monarchs and workers alike had seen
The glories of ancient Rome performed.
On an apron stage *The Tempest* stormed. |
| N | On seating all around the stage.
The people watched *King Lear* rage.
For an entry fee of tuppence
You could watch *MacBeth* get his come-uppence.
His most loved character the great Falstaff
Cavorted about and made everyone laugh. |
| N | Memories of childhood were food for Will's wit.
He recalled the woods where he used to sit
And made it the setting for *As You Like It*. |
| N | Forests and palaces, battles and shipwrecks,
The stuff of every Shakespeare text
Transported audience's imagination
In stories of triumph and damnation. |
| N | Shakespeare's mind was a treasure trove
Of tear-jerking stories of romantic love.
Mischievous fairies and treacherous imps
Made people laugh and cheer and wince. |
| N | The Wars of the Roses were grist to the mill
To the magnificent mind of Will.
He churned out plays of fury and force
(With a Tudor bias of course.) |
| N | Shakespeare's fame grew and grew
His salary was more attractive too.
This theatre company was such a success,
They built a new theatre of great finesse. |
| N | The Globe on the Thames' south bank was built
And every night the seats were filled
With many viewers eager to watch
Each new script from the top-notch
Theatre in the British Isles,
With tears and cheers and sighs and smiles. |
| N | Queen Elizabeth died in 1603
And King James moved from Scotland to be
The next King. Fortunately he
Loved the theatre as much as the Queen.
At the Globe he was often seen.
He became their patron, then
He renamed the group, The King's Men. |
| N | Now you're probably wondering
What, at this time, was happening |

To Shakespeare's wife and family.
He did go north tho' occasionally.
Acting was banned during Lent
So off to Stratford Shakespeare went.

N In 1592 there was plague.
Their knowledge of disease was rather vague.
London theatres had to be closed
For Londoners were not disposed
To risk catching the horrid disease.

N I'm sure Anne Shakespeare was quite pleased
When he returned home to the country
To spend some time with the family.

N A rich man now he could afford
A lovely big house in happy Stratford.
Suzanna, his daughter, was now nine,
A pretty girl who spent her time
In her brother and sister's company
Seven year old twins, Hamnet and Judy.

N The Shakespeare family were growing fast
But their pleasure did not last.
In 1596 a dreadful tragedy
Hit the Shakespeare family.

N Hamnet, their only son, died.
The Shakespeare family were beside
Themselves with grief for their boy of eleven.
They knelt and prayed he'd be safe in Heaven.

N In 1613 there was another disaster
A spark from a cannon spread a fire faster
Than the wind through the theatre.
To everyone's horror an hour later
Their lovely Globe was a heap of ash.
That for Shakespeare was the last
Episode of his writing career.
The theatre was rebuilt within a year.

N But Shakespeare now aged forty-nine,
A ripe old age at that time,
Retired from writing and went back home
To live with his daughters and his spouse
In New Place their beautiful big house.

N This was a time of sadness and joy.
His brothers died. He remembered as a boy
How they had played together for hours
In the woods, by the river and trees and flowers.

N His grand-daughter Elizabeth gave him great pleasure.
The happy old grand-dad now could treasure
Only three years of family life.
He caught a fever and although his wife
Tended him kindly, William passed away
On his birthday, St George's day.

N   Let us pray.
Oh God, thank you for the life of William Shakespeare and his wonderful gift of poetry and plays. We know we cannot all be great writers, but help us to make best use of our talents to benefit ourselves and others.

Secular

Chapter 9 Secular assemblies

Mother Teresa

1910 – 1997

Although today's Primary school pupils are too young to remember Mother Teresa, it is interesting for them to learn about a recent modern-day 'saint'.
This review of her life is in short, snappy scenes. The children can stand in a semi-circle at the back of the stage and come forward to play their part.

> **Characters**
>
> Agnes (Teresa)
> Drana, her mother
> Nikole, her father
> Aga, her sister
> Lazar, her brother
> Mother Dengal
> Man from the Council
> Voice on the train
> Doctor in the hospital
> Hindu priest
> Hindu protesters
> Sister Agnes (a young nun)
> Other nuns
> Policeman
> Pope
> 3 comperes
> King Olaf
> Lots of narrators, who double up with some of the parts above.

(*Everyone on stage to recite their parts in turn.*)

N	Good morning and welcome to our assembly. Today we would like to remember Mother Teresa of Calcutta. (*Show picture if you can. On the Internet there are lots, which can be put on screen.*)
N	Who was Mother Teresa of Calcutta?
N	Was she an Indian?
N	No she was European, from Macedonia.
N	What did she do?
N	She spent a large part of her life looking after people who were ill and dying in Calcutta. She was awarded the Nobel Peace prize in 1979.
N	Let us tell you about her.

N	Mother Teresa was born into a Christian family in Skopje on August 26th 1910. Her name was Agnes Bojaxhiu.

(Enter Drana, holding doll, being visited in hospital by Nikole, Aga, 7, and Lazar, 4.)

Nikole	Drana, another girl, how wonderful!
Aga	Let me see her, Mummy.
Lazar	She's beautiful, Mummy.
Nicole	What will we call her?
Drana	Agnes Gonxha. She will keep me busy when you are off travelling.

(They exit)

N	Agnes' father was a rich merchant. He travelled abroad on business and made lots of money. He was a generous man who gave a lot of his money away to the poor. When he returned he always thrilled his children with stories of the countries he had visited on business.

(Enter Agnes, Drana, Lazar and Aga)

Agnes	*(Now about 5 years old)* You've got a lot of food there, Mummy. Who is coming to dinner?
Drana	I don't know. I'm sure some people will turn up.
Aga	Why do so many people come to our house to eat? We have guests every day.
Lazar	We don't even know who they are.
Drana	Some are relatives, but all of them are our people.
Agnes	But often you do not know who they are.
Aga	Why do you feed strangers, Mummy?
Drana	Because they are starving. We are all members of the family of God.
N	When Agnes was eight, tragedy struck the family.

(Enter man from the council)

Man from Council
Mrs Bojaxhiu, I am so sorry I have terrible news. Nikole came to the council meeting, but after the meeting we had dinner and Nikole collapsed and died. I am so sorry.

(The family cry)

N	The Bojaxhiu family were no longer rich, but they were still generous. Drana could not keep her husband's business going but she started dressmaking to keep the family. Still people came to the house for their evening meal.
N	Agnes was clever and worked hard at school. She admired her mother's generous nature and decided to become a missionary in India.
Drana	Are you sure you want to become a missionary, Agnes?
Agnes	Yes mother, I'm quite sure.
Drana	I am very proud of you but are you sure you want to give up your chance to be

	married and have a family and your own home. If you go into this you must go with your whole heart or not at all.
Agnes	I'm quite sure it is what I want to do, Mummy.
Drana	How will you get to India?
Agnes	I have already spoken to the priest. He has advised me to go to Ireland and join the Loreto Sisters in Dublin. They will train me and send me to their convent in Calcutta and prepare me for the work.
Lazar	Oh don't go, Agnes. If you start that sort of life you will never come back here.
Agnes	You think you are important because you serve a king of two million people. I am going to serve the king of the whole world. Which one of us is doing the better job?
N	Agnes left Skopje in 1928 when she was eighteen years old. She travelled with another girl called Betika Kajnc overland through Austria, Switzerland, France and England to Dublin. While the two young women were in Dublin they learnt English and began their lives as nuns.
N	Agnes took on a new name: Sister Mary Teresa. Soon she was off again by boat to India. The journey took weeks. One day a letter arrived at the Bojaxhiu family home.

(Enter Drana, Lazar and Aga)

Drana	Lazar, Aga. There is a letter here from Agnes. *(Opens letter and reads)* Dear Mum, Aga and Lazar, We had a long sea journey from Dublin to Colombo. It was so exciting to sail past France and Spain and across the Mediterranean Sea. I thought of you all as we passed by Italy and Greece. We arrived in Colombo on the Island of Ceylon on 27th December. There is great poverty there although the land is rich in tropical plants. We then moved on to Madras. The poverty is dreadful, the worst I have ever seen. So many people have no homes, no food and almost no clothing. They live on the streets sleeping on mats of palm leaves or even on the bare, filthy ground. Now we are in Bengal and have arrived at Darjeeling at the bottom of the Himalayas. We have two years to learn the local languages like Hindi and perfect our English. We also have to learn about the way of life of India. We are very happy that we have got here at last and are looking forward to working. I am training to be a teacher. I shall also learn to look after the sick in a hospital. I think of you all often and send you all my love, Teresa

(The family exit. Teresa and pupils enter.)

N	In 1931, after Sister Teresa had finished her Novitiate, the first part of her training as a nun, she went off to the poverty stricken Calcutta to teach in St Mary's High School.

(Teresa looks around the room in disgust and speaks to her pupils.)

Teresa	This school is in a disgusting state. It is filthy. Let's get it clean. Who's going to join me?
N	Sister Teresa rolled up her sleeves and found brushes and dusters and buckets of water and they swept and washed and polished until the classroom was clean.

(Teresa and pupils mime.)

N   Sister Teresa loved her pupils and enjoyed her work but she was heart-broken about the poverty of the people.

(Exit Teresa and pupils. Enter her family.)

Drana   Aga, Lazar, I have another letter from Agnes

Dear Mother, Aga and Lazar,
I hope you are all well. We have settled in to our school work. When we arrived there were only about fifty children coming, but now there are four hundred. We have had to divide up our large school room to make up classes with dozens of children in each class.
The children love coming to school and it is hardly surprising. On Sundays I visit them in their homes and I can hardly believe the poverty in which these poor children struggle to survive. Each family lives in a single room about two metres by one and a half metres. The ceiling is so low that even I cannot stand up straight, and the doorway is so narrow that it is hard to squeeze in and out.
I think that it must be a great relief for them to come to school and feel comfortable and do something interesting.
I send you all my love,
Teresa

(Exit family. Teresa enters and sits down.)

N   In 1937, when Sister Teresa was twenty-seven, she took her final vows as a nun and was immediately made Headteacher of St Mary's High School where she worked for a further nine years. During this time World War II was raging.

N   Once every year, Sister Teresa returned to Darjeeling for a short rest. In 1946, the year after the war ended, Sister Teresa was sitting on the train to Darjeeling when she heard a voice calling to her.

Voice   Leave the convent and your school and go and help the poor of Calcutta by living among them.

N   Teresa was certain this was the voice of God so she got permission from her Bishop and the Pope to start a hospital for the poor.

N   Before that, she had to go to Patna to a missionary hospital to have a crash course in nursing. She had a lot to learn.

(Enter Teresa and Mother Dengal)

Mother Dengal
     Why have you left your school, Teresa?

Teresa   I was sitting on a train when God spoke to me, telling me to go and help the poor on the streets of Calcutta.

Mother Dengal
     How will you go about it when you return?

Teresa I will start a new order of nuns. We will be called the Missionaries of Charity. We will have to find a building to use as our hospital. We must make sure we are as poor as the patients so we will eat only rice and salt.

Mother Dengal
And what use would that be? Do you want to make your nuns as ill as the poor so that they are unable to help them? Do you want your nuns to die before their patients so they won't be strong and healthy to look after the poor for God?

(Exit Mother Dengal)

N India was now an independent state, free of British rule, but the country was very unsettled and there were many refugees. In 1948, Teresa became an Indian citizen. She set up her own order of nuns, and she was joined by one of her ex-pupils from St Mary's High School. Her ex-pupil took the name of Sister Agnes in honour of Teresa because it had been her name. They were called the Missionaries of Charity and so Teresa now became known as Mother Teresa.

N They started with a hut but soon they needed a larger building. A wealthy Muslim sold them his house at a low price which the church paid. One day Mother Teresa was walking out of the local hospital.

(Woman on the ground dying, approached by Teresa and a nun.)

Agnes This poor woman is dying.
(Chases rats and flies off her body)

She is so weak she cannot brush away the rats and flies on her body.

Teresa You stay and comfort her. I will go inside and get her a bed.

(Teresa moves across the stage to a doctor inside the hospital.)

Teresa Doctor, there is a woman dying just outside the hospital. She is lying on the street, so weak she cannot even move the rats and flies off herself. You must give her a bed.

Doctor But you have to pay to stay here.

Teresa You know this woman cannot pay. She will be dead within a day or two. Surely you can find enough kindness in your heart to take her in and let her die in peace and comfort.

Doctor All right. I'm sure we can find her a bed somewhere.

N This made Mother Teresa realize that the town needed a building where people who were dying could finish their days in comfort, so she went to the council and persuaded the officials to give her a hostel near the local Hindu temple of Kali. In 1952 the missionaries opened their hospital for the dying.

Agnes This is wonderful, Mother. We can bring people here to help them through their last days.

Teresa We will call it the Place of the Pure Heart.

(Enter the Hindu priest.)

Hindu Priest Why have you opened this place?

Agnes	We want to give a home to people who are dying so that they can be comfortable for the last few weeks of their lives.
Hindu Priest	But we already have a place for that. Look next door at our temple. We look after Hindus who are dying. We do not need you here.
Teresa	But our hospital is for everyone. Hindus, Muslims, Christians, anyone will be welcomed here.
Hindu Priest	I do not believe you. I believe you are using your hospital to turn Hindu people into Christians.
Agnes	I assure you we do not try to ...
Hindu Priest	I don't care what you say. I wish you would go away.

(Two nuns rush in, frightened.)

1st Nun	Mother, we have been pelted in the streets with sticks and stones.
2nd Nun	How can anyone do this to us?
Hindu Priest	They throw stones at you because they know that you are here to take people away from their own religion.

(Exit all)

N	The people in the neighbourhood protested to the police about the nuns and their hospital for the dying.

(Priest and protesters stride in to the police station.)

Hindu Priest	We don't want that Christian hospital next to our temple.
Policeman	Why not? Mother Teresa and her nuns are doing an excellent job. They take people who are dying off the streets and bring them to their hospital and make them comfortable.
1st Protester	We don't need them to do that. We have a hospital for our own people.
2nd Protester	But The Place of the Pure Heart takes in dying people of all religions to help them to die peacefully.
3rd Protester	Nonsense! They are only taking them in because they want to make them Christians.
Policeman	All right, I will close down The Place of the Pure Heart, but only on the condition that you all go home and persuade your mothers and wives and sisters to do that work which Mother Teresa and the Missionaries of Charity are now doing.

(They exit. Enter Mother Teresa and the Hindu priest who lies down.)

N	And that finished that argument. Mother Teresa and her nuns were allowed to continue their work. One day Mother Theresa was passing the Hindu Temple of Kali. The Hindu priest was lying on the steps.
Teresa	You poor man, you need help.
Hindu Priest	I have cholera. Everyone is frightened to come near me in case they get it from me.

Teresa	Agnes, help me. We can take him home with us.

(They help him up)

Agnes	There is a free bed in the hospital. We can look after you.
N	They took him to The Place of the Pure Heart and nursed him until he died. They had not realized that he was the priest who had tried to close their hospital down.
N	When the local people discovered that they had looked after their dying priest, they stopped protesting.
N	Next, Mother Teresa opened a home for abandoned babies who had been thrown onto rubbish heaps.
N	Mother Teresa then took up the case of the lepers, people who are ill with leprosy. It is a nasty disease which makes a body waste away and the person look ugly. Some types of leprosy are infectious and so people are afraid to go near lepers.
N	Mother Teresa's work was now growing so fast that she was well known throughout India. In 1964 Pope VI came to India and visited her.

(Enter Pope)

Pope	Mother Teresa, your work is wonderful. You have done more than anyone in India to help the ill and dying. What can I do to help you in your excellent work?
Teresa	We need funds, Your Holiness.
Pope	I have been driven round in this very expensive car while I have been here. When my trip is over I shall give it to you and I am sure you can put it to good use.
Teresa	Thank you Your Holiness. It will be used for our work.
N	The car was raffled and they made five times as much as it was worth.
N	With the help of money given by people who were interested and a retired doctor who was willing to work without pay, Mother Teresa and her people opened a mobile clinic for lepers.
N	In the 1970s Mother Teresa became known all over the world. She was given awards and prizes.
1st Compere	The winner of the 1971 Pope John XXIII Peace Prize is Mother Teresa of Calcutta.

(Applause as Mother Teresa comes on to take her prize and they move to the back of the stage for the 2nd compere.)

2nd Compere The winner of the 1971 Good Samaritan award is Mother Teresa of Calcutta.

(Applause as Mother Teresa comes on to take her prize and they move to the back of the stage for the 3rd compere.)

3rd Compere The winner of the 1971 Joseph P Kennedy foundation award is Mother Teresa of Calcutta.

(Applause as Mother Teresa comes on to take her prize and they move to the back.)

N	The greatest award of all came in 1979.
King Olaf	It gives me great pleasure to award the 1979 Nobel Peace Prize to Mother Teresa of Calcutta.

Teresa	Personally I am unworthy. I accept in the name of the poor because I believe that by giving me the prize you have recognized the presence of the poor in the world.
N	Mother Teresa asked them to cancel the celebration banquet and give the money instead to her hospitals.
N	Today there are hospitals run by the Missionaries of Charity all over the world in
N	Venezuela,
N	Sri Lanka,
N	Tanzania,
N	Rome,
N	Australia.
N	On 5th September 1997, Mother Teresa died peacefully just a few days after her 87th birthday.
N	When Mother Teresa died, these sentences were found in her own handwriting, on the wall beside her bed.
N	People are often unreasonable, illogical or self-centred. Forgive them anyway.
N	If you are successful, you will be sure to make some false friends and some true enemies. Be successful anyway.
N	If you are honest and frank, people may cheat you. Be honest and frank anyway.
N	What you spend years building, someone could destroy overnight. Build anyway.
N	If you find serenity and happiness others may be jealous. Be happy anyway.
N	The good you do today people will often forget tomorrow. Be good anyway.
N	Give the world the best you have and it may never be enough. Give the world the best you've got anyway.
N	You see, in the end it is between you and God. It was never between you and them anyway.
N	Let us pray. Oh God, we can never live up to the amazing example of Mother Teresa, but please help us to follow her example of kindness and care for all people of every race. Help us always to be willing to help anyone in difficulty or in need of a friend.

Secular

Chapter 9 Secular assemblies

Bonfire Night

5th November 1605

Every year children look forward to bonfire parties and burning the guy, but many do not know the origin of the tradition. This is an enjoyable way for a class to teach the story to the school.

> **Characters**
>
> Queen Elizabeth
> Conspirators
> Robert Catesby
> Thomas Wintour
> Thomas Percy
> Jack Wright
> Robert Wintour
> Kit Wright
> Robert Keyes
> Thomas Bates
> John Grant (non-speaking)
> Ambrose Rookwood (non-speaking)
> Francis Tresham (non-speaking)
> Everard Digby (non-speaking)
> Guy Fawkes (non-speaking)
> Servant (non-speaking)
> Stranger on the street
> Lord Monteagle
> Guards (non-speaking)
> Lots of narrators, who double up as many of the non-speaking parts.

N   Look back in time over four centuries
          To the end of the Tudor dynasty.
          Queen Elizabeth sat on the throne
          And England was stronger than ever known.

(During the next two verses pupils, in the background, mime sailing, painting, playing musical instruments and writing.)

N   William Shakespeare's theatre thrived.
          The Armada had come but the English survived.
          The great explorers had sailed the world
          And the English flag had been unfurled
          In distant lands across the sea,
          And the English enjoyed prosperity.

N   The great Renaissance had touched our land.

	There were artists and writers and musicians grand. And religious changes swept through England.
N	There'd been plots to kill the Protestant Queen But fortunately the plotters had all been seen Off to the tower and off with their heads! So the queen's supporters slept sound in their beds.
N	But all was not perfect, I'm sorry to say. Tolerance was still not the order of the day. There was sometimes enmity Between Catholic and Protestant families.
N	When plots were discovered against the queen Suspicion once more arose between The Protestants and the Catholics. This put the queen in a fix.
Queen	I want a peaceful kingdom,
N	she said. But persecution raised its ugly head. Queen Elizabeth died in 1603. The Catholics had waited patiently.
N	Down from Scotland came her cousin James Hotfoot to London to make his claims To the crown of England, he was our next king, But sadly it didn't change a thing.
N	Although James' mother was the Catholic Mary, Life has a way of being contrary. Still the Catholics felt persecuted. Robert Catesby said

(Enter Catesby)

Catesby	We've pussyfooted Around, waiting far too long. Now is the time to take a strong And violent action to make a stand And rid our green and pleasant land Of this Protestant king quite quick.
N	And he hatched a nasty, explosive trick.

(Enter Thomas Wintour, Thomas Percy and Jack Wright)

Catesby	Come here Thomas Wintour, Thomas Percy, Jack Wright. It's time to quash this problem outright. Too long we have suffered from persecution. I have found the perfect solution. This autumn at the opening of Parliament We'll take a stand to make them lament The years they oppressed the Catholic population. We'll send a shiver through the nation.

              Let's rent a room 'neath the House of Lords
              And fill it up with deadly hoards
              Of gunpowder barrels, and on the day,
              We'll blast the lot of them far away.

Thomas Wintour
              But are you sure the plan will work?
              Can we find an expert who will not shirk
              From such a vile and murderous task?
              Who could do it? Whom could we ask?

Percy   Guy Fawkes is the man, though he's not one of us.
              He's a loyal Catholic so we can trust
              Him to join our conspiracy.
              He has fought many years across the sea
              In Holland and Spain as a mercenary.

Jack Wright He's an expert with gunpowder,
              And no man has shouted louder
              To restore the rights of Catholics.
              And he won't mind the politics.
              Ask him soon. I'm sure he'll fix
              The barrels for us, one by one
              And blow them all to kingdom come.

Thomas Wintour
              He sounds just the man, I think.
              Let's invite him for a drink.

N   They wrote a note for a servant to take
              To Fawkes to meet them at the Duck and Drake.
              They met Fawkes in the pub in the Strand.

(Guy Fawkes meets the four conspirators and they stand in a semicircle facing the audience.)

Percy   My friend we know how to rid our land
              Of persecution, but we need your skill.
              Will you join with us to kill
              The Royal Family and all the MPs
              At Parliament's opening, please.

N   So Guy Fawkes joined the murderous crew.

(The other conspirators enter and shake hands with Catesby and the others and enlarge the semicircle, facing the audience.)

              Robert Wintour, Kit Wright and Robert Keyes too.
              Thomas Bates, John Grant, brought the number to ten
              Ambrose Rookwood, Francis Tresham, Everard Digby, then
              There were thirteen conspirators waiting happily
              To murder their MPs and royal family.

Robert Wintour
              Absolute secrecy is a must.
              Not one of us should dare to trust
              A single person with this plot
              If we're caught, we'll all be shot.

Kit Wright	You know, men, a few miles north of the city, On Hampstead Heath there is a pretty Tall and grassy hill with a view For miles around you can see to The River Thames and the Parliament.
Keyes	That's right friends, it is my intent To go there on the day to see This job carried out successfully.
Bates	A great idea! Oh what a joke! To watch the place go up in smoke.

(Conspirators mime carrying barrels of gunpowder into the basement.)

N	And so the plans were carefully made And one by one the barrels laid In the cellar beneath the House of Lords, A deathly lot beneath floorboards.
N	Now nobody knows how it came about But the nasty plot was found out.
N	There was a loyal Catholic, Lord Monteagle The most honest and upright of people. The day before Parliament was due to meet, His servant went out for a stroll in the street.

(Servant walks down the street and stranger slips him a note.)

N	A stranger approached him looking worried.
Stranger	Give this note to your master.

(He rushes away. Servant takes the note to Lord Monteagle.)

N	The servant hurried Home at once to show his boss. Lord Monteagle was at a loss To know who could have written it, Before Parliament was due to sit.
Lord Monteagle *(Reading)*	Do not go near Parliament tomorrow. To avoid the tragedy and sorrow. An unspeakable disaster will take place And shock the entire English race.
N	The good Lord Monteagle raised the alarm. And stopped the conspirators causing harm. They searched the cellars of Westminster Palace And stopped the plotters' act of malice.

(Guards walk into the cellar and take Guy Fawkes and a few conspirators off-stage. The guards then return to stage to be narrators.)

N   Guy Fawkes was first to feel the pain
He was tortured over and over again.
A ruthless man, he was also brave
They asked him but he never gave
The names of the other men away.
But they were rounded up anyway.

N   One by one they were put to death.
The English people held their breath
Knowing that there could have been
A murder of the King and Queen
The Prince of Wales and all the MPs.
They all gave thanks for their safe release.

N   And now today, each November
In Parliament they still remember
To have the cellars thoroughly checked
To stop the place from being wrecked.

N   These events took place in 1605 over 400 years ago. Today no one takes seriously the idea that someone would blow up Parliament.

N   However the event is commemorated with bonfire parties. People make a dummy called a guy and burn it on a huge fire in a local park or large garden. Often people then have a party with fireworks and a barbecued supper.

N   Let us pray.
Oh God, we thank you that the terrible act of murder and destruction did not take place. Thank you for making us people who accept other people's religion and allow everyone to live peacefully.
This week many of us will be going to parties with bonfires and fireworks. Please help us to remember the importance of playing safely so we can enjoy the fun without anyone being hurt.

Chapter 9 Secular assemblies

Bishop Gregory and St Augustine

540 – 604 (Gregory)

An assembly on St Augustine, one of the lesser known saints, may not seem like an obvious choice for a Key Stage 2 assembly. If studying the history unit of Invaders and Settlers, this one is an effective way to reinforce your lessons on how Christianity returned to Britain in the Dark Ages.

Characters

Gregory
Bishop of Rome
Servant
Lawyer
Slaves
Man in the market
Abbot
Augustine
Bishop of Rome
Monks
King Ethelbert
Queen Berta
Princess Ethelburga
King Edwin
Old man
Lots of narrators

(Narrators on stage to start. They can move forward to play their part and then move to the side of the stage or off-stage.)

N	Our story starts many centuries ago. The exact year, we really don't know. In the 6th century A.D. Far away in Italy, The Roman Empire was no longer Fighting wars and growing stronger.
N	The mighty empire had declined. Only the buildings were there to remind Everyone of their glorious past. Their temples and amphitheatres would last For centuries to be used and admired. While most of their army was long retired.
N	In Rome lived a man named Gregory, A wealthy man who lived in luxury.

	He studied law and eventually, Gregory became a judge.
N	Every day he used to trudge From home to court and back again, Sitting at the trials of wicked men. But really judgement wasn't his thing.
N	He preferred to read and pray and sing Hymns and psalms. He was deeply religious. Preferring peace and calm to the prestigious Life of a judge in the city of Rome. One day when he arrived home, Some sad news was awaiting him.

(Enter servant and lawyer and Gregory from the opposite side.)

Servant	Your poor father became ill today. I'm sorry sir. He's just passed away.
Lawyer	You know, Gregory, what this means to you. He has left you all his money. You are now a very wealthy man indeed. You have enough money to last for the rest of your life.
Gregory	That doesn't mean a lot to me. I don't want a life of idle luxury and I don't want to spend all day listening to the work of bad men. I'd rather give my life to God and work in the church. I shall give it all away and go into a monastery.

(They exit)

N	So Gregory, the most generous man in the city, Gave all his money away to charity. He packed all his bags and went off at once To join the Benedictine monks.

(Gregory enters with Abbot who shows him to his room.)

Abbot	Gregory, this room will be yours. You will get up every day at dawn. There is plenty of cold water to wash and then go straight to church for morning prayers. After that you will have a glass of milk and work for two hours in the vegetable garden. Breakfast of bread and milk will be in the dining hall and you will work for the rest of the day with short breaks for meals. In the evening you will join everyone in church for evening prayers and then you will go to your room to read your Bible until dark. You will be allowed one candle each week. Use it wisely.
Gregory	Thank you Abbot.
N	But Gregory was not in dismay He played his part, every day. He was happy to work and sing and pray. So he did his work with his Christian brothers. A kindly man, he was loved by the others.
N	A new monk named Augustine came one day. To join in and live the monastic way.
Gregory	Welcome to the Benedictine Abbey. I hope you will enjoy your new life.
Augustine	I'm sure I shall. I'm looking forward to being away from the bustle of everyday life.
N	The years slipped by and the abbot died.

	Now the monks had to decide Who'd be the next Benedictine Abbot. This was something to talk about.

(The monks all put their hands together and bow to Gregory who bows in return.)

N	The brothers choose our Gregory As a man of goodness and charity, Fit to be their next Abbot. So Gregory put on the leader's habit.

(They exit. Gregory enters market and sees slave boys at one side.)

N	Gregory used to go out of the monastery. One day in the market he happened to see Some handsome boys with fair skin, Chained up to a post and all penned in.
Gregory	Who are those little boys over there? They are light skinned and fair haired. They have blue eyes. They can't be from anywhere round the Mediterranean Sea.
Man in market	Those slaves-boys are from Angleland. They are little Angles.
Gregory	I think they are Angels, not Angles. It is dreadful to think that this country still has slavery.
Man	The Angles can be a savage lot, you know.
Gregory	Then I think I'd love to go to Angleland and teach the people about Jesus Christ. It would be wonderful to go to a pagan country and make it into a Christian country. I think I'll visit the Bishop of Rome to ask if I can go there.

(They exit)

N	So Gregory shot off to see the man To explain his exciting plan. The bishop was looking rather ill, But he was pleased to see our Gregory, still.

(Enter Gregory and Bishop)

Bishop	Gregory. It's a pleasure to see you. What can I do for you?
Gregory	I have seen some slave boys from Angleland in the market. They tell me that Angleland is full of pagans. I would love to go there and preach the gospel. Think how wonderful it would be to turn it into a Christian country. I'd love to take a group of my monks there. I have come to ask your permission to go.
Bishop	That's a wonderful idea, Gregory. Of course you may go. I shall pray for you to have a safe journey and convert many people to Christianity.

(They exit)

N	So Gregory, delighted, hurried back Home to tell his friends to pack. Their luggage wasn't hard to bear Just a little food for them to share.

(Gregory, Augustine and four monks start walking off the stage and round the hall.)

N	They all walked north through Italy, Each night sleeping in a different monastery. And after each night of bed and board, The happy band got back on the road.
N	But their well-laid plan did not last long. After only three days the happy old throng Of monks were surprised to be overtaken By a messenger with news that left them shaking.

(Enter messenger)

Messenger The Bishop is dead. You have to return to Rome. Abbot Gregory will have to be the next Bishop.

Gregory This is terrible news, but we'll have to return to Rome.

(They turn around and retrace their steps.)

N	So sadly the band of monks turned round. To travel back o'er the same old ground. And three days later they reached their home And Gregory became the new Bishop of Rome.
N	But Gregory never forgot the slaves. There's a place in Heaven for one who saves People from pagan and heathen ways.
N	One day he sent for Augustine.

(Enter Gregory and Augustine)

Gregory Augustine, I have never forgotten those slave boys from Angleland. I want you to go there. Go back to the monastery and pack up again and go off to Angleland.

Augustine All right, we'll go as soon as we can.

(Augustine and five monks pack up and start walking.)

N	So Augustine organized his happy band. And they set off walking overland. They journeyed through Italy and into France. They stopped at a tavern and quite by chance, They met a merchant who'd stopped for the night. His news gave the monks a dreadful fright.

Merchant You look like men with a mission. Where are you going?

Augustine We are going to Angleland.

Merchant Why on earth do you want to go to that dreadful land?

Augustine To convert the people to Christianity, of course.

Merchant You must be mad. They are a bunch of awful savages. They will kill you as soon as they look at you. There's no way you will win anyone for God in that place. Your wisest move would be to go back to Italy and leave the savages in Angleland alone.

Augustine What do you think, brothers? Should we go on or should we go home?

1st Monk	I think we should go on, God will look after us.
2nd Monk	I'd like to go home. What is the point of getting ourselves killed. We would be no use to God then.
3rd Monk	I want to go on. Life is more exciting travelling to a new land and taking on a challenge than the routine humdrum life of the monastery.
4th Monk	But suppose this merchant is right.
3rd Monk	Suppose he's wrong.
5th Monk	What will Bishop Gregory say when we return to Rome?
1st Monk	He'll be so disappointed that we didn't even try to get to Angleland.
2nd Monk	He'd be even more disappointed if he got news that we'd all been killed.
Augustine	I think we need to have a vote on it. All who want to go on to Angleland, raise your hand.

(1st and 3rd monks raise their hands)

Augustine   Who wants to go back to Rome?

(All the others raise their hands.)

Augustine   All right. We'll go home.

(Augustine and monks turn round and walk back.)

N   And so the band of missionaries turned round
And on the road to Rome were bound.
They arrived tired out with very sore feet.
And off to the palace they went to meet
Bishop Gregory to explain the position.
Why they failed in their holy mission.

(Enter Gregory to meet the monks.)

Augustine	We were so scared, Bishop. The monks were afraid to go on.
Gregory	Why were you frightened?
2nd Monk	Because the cloth merchant said that the Angles were bloodthirsty savages who would kill us soon as we landed and they would not even let us begin to tell the Gospel.
Gregory	That is why you have to go there! To stop them being bloodthirsty and killing people. They need the word of God to teach them to live in peace.
4th Monk	We are still frightened.
Gregory	Don't tell me you let the word of one cloth merchant put you off the work of God? Don't you realize that God always watches over everyone who is doing his work. Go back on the road and God will look after you. He will keep you safe and when you arrive there he will look after you. Go back to Angleland and do God's work.
Augustine	All right, Bishop, we'll go.
N	So the monks went home and washed and slept
Their promise to Gregory had to be kept.

> They packed again and off they went.
> Unsure and anxious about being sent.
> But a few months later they arrived in Kent.

(Monks step off the boat and look around at the new land.)

Augustine We've arrived at last. I feared we'd never get here.

2nd Monk *(Aside)* I hoped we'd never get here.

Augustine Let's all gather round and say a prayer.
God our Father, thank you for bringing us safely here. Please keep us safe so that we can do your work and bring these people to You.

Monks Amen.

(Enter messenger)

Messenger I am a messenger from the court of King Ethelbert of Kent. He wants to meet you.

Augustine That's great! We'll go at once.

N And so their prayers were answered quickly.
The monks shot off to the palace slickly.
And would you believe it, their luck was in.
Queen Berta was already a Christian.

(Enter King Ethelbert and Queen Berta)

King Ethelbert
> Welcome strangers, drink and eat.
> Sit down, take the weight off your feet.
> We don't get many strangers here.
> Tell me your purpose. I want to hear
> Where you have come from? What is your mission?

Augustine We have come, hoping for your kind permission
To preach the Gospel in your land.
We have brought good news for every man
And woman. We bring you Christianity.
A way of life for all humanity.

(They all sit down and mime speaking and praying.)

N So all night long the Queen and King
Listened well to everything
That Augustine had to say.
They believed the monks could show the way
To gain eternal life. Then they prayed.

King Ethelbert
> Thank you for coming. I am persuaded
> That this kingdom will be up-graded
> From now on I shall join my wife
> And we'll all follow your way of life.

N And so the happy monks had won
Their first converts. Their first job was done.
The grateful king gave a command

	To his men to build churches on his land.
N	The monks went off in great haste And built a church near the place Where they had first arrived in Kent. To the monks this all seemed Heaven-sent.

(They mime building)

N	Having got started, they were in a hurry. So off they went to Canterbury. Another church was soon erected. This luck was better than they expected.
King Ethelbert	Our daughter, Princess Ethelburga is about to marry Edwin, the King of Northumbria. I would like one of your monks to come north with us and try to persuade Edwin to become a Christian.
Augustine	Yes, of course, we'd be honoured.
N	Augustine and the monks were so excited That one of them had been invited To travel north. It was not expected. And Brother Paulinus was selected.
N	So the faithful monk packed up his kit. There really wasn't much of it. And the band of travellers went forth Up to Angleland's rainy north.

(Edwin sits down with Ethelburga beside him. Her parents sit beside her and Paulinus in front of them. A few other people are in the group, including an old man. Paulinus mimes talking. They mime watching the bird flying in and out.)

N	And after the marriage of Ethelburga and Edwin Paulinus was called to talk to him. Paulinus told the story of Jesus' life Of the resurrection and everlasting life.
N	But Edwin was not quite convinced. Through a window a little bird inched Its way inside King Edwin's hall. It flapped its wings and looked at all The people sitting round the room. It flew around and began to zoom Out of the window and away again. The king watched for a few seconds and asked his men,
King Edwin	What do you think men? I'm not sure why We should give up our own gods. Is this worth a try?

(He turns and looks at an old man sitting in silence.)

Old man	You know, it seems to me that our short lives here are like that little bird's flight. The world lasts for thousands of years but we are only here for about forty or fifty. Then we do not know what happens to us or where we will go to then. I think that we should listen to our good friend Paulinus because this may be the only chance

we have of ever having life after death.

N   And so King Edwin followed the trend
From then on, he became Paulinus' friend.
He encouraged him to carry on his mission
And just like Ethelbert, he gave permission
For churches to be built everywhere
And all his people were encouraged to share
The Good News of Jesus' life and teaching.

N   Paulinus spent all his life preaching.
And Christianity spread across Angleland
His church in York was simply grand.
And other monks took up the call
And soon spread the word of God to all.

N   Let us pray.
Oh God, we thank you for the lives of brave men like St Augustine who brought Christianity back to Britain. Whichever religion we follow, help us to practise it and live peacefully with people of all religions.

Chapter 9 Secular assemblies

Charles Dickens

1812 – 1870

Charles Dickens was arguably the most popular novelist of the 19th Century and worthy to be included in a book of assemblies. His books, in their original form, are difficult for most Primary school children to read, but there are many abridged versions on the market and children who are introduced to them early can develop a love of his excellent and insightful works.

Characters

Charles Dickens (as a child)
Charles Dickens (as a man)
John Dickens, his father
Elizabeth Dickens, his mother
Dickens children
Policeman
Oliver Twist
Mr Bumble
4 gentlemen of the Board in the workhouse
Workhouse man
Boys in the workhouse } These can double up.
Boys in the school   }
David Copperfield
Mr Creakle
Mr Squeers
Mrs Squeers
Lots of narrators who can also be the characters above to share the lines out evenly.

(Across the middle of the stage is a line of tables with chairs behind them. One table is at the side for Dickens the man to sit. All of the children on the stage as narrators to start.)

N	Good morning and welcome to our assembly.
N	What has each of these got in common?
N	Pickwick Papers
N	A Christmas Carol
N	The Cricket on the Hearth
N	Barnaby Rudge
N	Oliver Twist
N	David Copperfield
N	Dombey and Son

N	A Tale of Two Cities
N	Nicholas Nickleby
N	Bleak House
N	Our Mutual Friend
N	The Old Curiosity Shop
N	Great Expectations
N	Little Dorrit
N	Martin Chuzzlewit
N	Hard Times
N	The Mystery of Edwin Drood

(Allow a child in the audience to answer.)

N   That's right. They are all books by Charles Dickens.

N   Today we are going to tell you about Charles Dickens, one of England's finest story writers.

N   Charles Dickens was born in Portsea on the south coast of England on 7th February 1812 to John and Elizabeth Dickens. John Dickens was a clerk in a Naval Office. He was a happy man who always looked on the bright side, but he was hopeless at handling money and often got into debt. When Charles Dickens wrote David Copperfield, he used his father as a model for Mr Micawber.

N   His mother was a very funny woman and Dickens modelled the character of Mrs Nickleby on her in his book, Nicholas Nickleby.

(Narrators move to the sides of the stage. During the next several speeches Charles, the boy, mimes the action. For the rest of the assembly, Charles, the man, sits at a table at the side and writes.)

N   When he was two years old the family moved to Chatham and young Charles spent several happy years exploring the dockyard and the beautiful Kent countryside round the town. This came out years later in 'David Copperfield' when he described the young child stopping to sleep by an old canon on his way to Kent.

N   One day, while out walking, he saw a beautiful house called Gad's Hills Place. Charles Dickens thought it a wonderful house and longed to own it.

N   Charles had a wonderful imagination and also loved reading. This happy time came to an end when the Dickens family, who now had several children, moved to London.

(Lots of children move onto the stage and stand around in groups chatting while young Charles wanders around lost and anxious.)

N   One day when he was nine years old, he got lost in London and wandered around on his own. He recalled this event by putting it into his book, 'Dombey and Son' when Dombey's daughter got lost and had a terrifying time wandering around alone in the bustling and dangerous city.

(Exit all. Mr and Mrs Dickens and their family enter and sit down at the tables and there is a knock at the door. Mr Dickens answers and in comes a policeman who beckons them to come with them and they go out leaving young Charles Dickens alone.)

N In London the Dickens family lived in a small dingy house in Camden and John Dickens got into debt again. He and most of his family were taken off to Marshalsea Debtors' Prison. So just before his twelfth birthday, Charles was sent to work in a blacking factory for six shillings a week.

(Charles, the adult continues to write while young Charles looks around anxiously.)

N The factory was dark and dirty and had rats running around and Charles had a three mile walk to work. He hated it but used the experience in his book David Copperfield, when David was sent to work in a blacking factory. Eventually Dicken's father came out of prison and Charles was sent to school for a short time and then out to work in a solicitor's office on High Holborn. There are still solicitors' offices there today behind Chancery Lane tube station. When he worked there he met lots of characters whom he remembered and used in books like Bleak House.

(Young Charles exits and Charles, the man, sitting at a table writing, occasionally looks up to think and has a contented expression.)

N Dickens loved writing and was determined to make a career out of it so he learnt shorthand and got a job as a newspaper reporter at the age of eighteen. He had to travel around the countryside by coach to go to the places to report back to his newspaper. His descriptions of these uncomfortable rides come up in his book 'A Tale of Two Cities'.

N Dickens loved reading and writing short stories. He began writing stories under the pen name of 'Boz' and they were published in magazines and newspapers. He then went on to write novels and became the greatest novelist of the 19th Century. His books are still popular today.

N Charles Dickens was a man who thought about the many bad things in England at his time. He put these into his books to let everyone know how dreadful some things were. The worst of these was the workhouse which was a house for poor people who had nowhere else to go. Each workhouse was run by a board of people in the parish. The people who ran the workhouses did not care for the poor and treated them cruelly.

N In Oliver Twist he showed everyone how cruelly people were treated.

N We will show you some scenes from 'Oliver Twist'. Oliver Twist was born in the workhouse and farmed out to a woman of the parish who looked after him until he was nine and old enough to go back to the workhouse to work. The woman of the parish showed him no love and fed him as little as she could.

N On the day he returned, Mr Bumble the beadle, a church officer brought him in to meet the Board, a group of men who looked after the workhouse and cared nothing for the people in it.

(A group of four men, looking stern, sit behind the tables and Mr Bumble comes in holding Oliver by the collar. The child is barefoot and looks terrified.)

Mr Bumble Oliver, bow to the Board.

(Oliver looks around scared and unsure who are the Board. Mr Bumble points him in the right direction and he bows nervously.)

1st Gentleman of the Board
    What's your name, boy?

(Oliver stammers, unable to speak.)

    Boy, listen to me. You know that you're an orphan, I suppose.

Oliver   What's that, sir?

2nd Gentleman of the Board
    The boy is a fool. I thought he was.

1st Gentleman of the Board
    Hush. You know that you have no father or mother and that you were brought up by the parish, don't you?

Oliver   Yes sir.

2nd Gentleman of the Board
    What are you crying for?

3rd Gentleman of the Board
    I hope you say your prayers every night, and pray for the people who take care of you and feed you – like a Christian.

Oliver   *(Stammering)* Yes sir.

1st Gentleman of the Board
    Well you have come here to be educated and taught a useful trade.

3rd Gentleman of the Board
    So tomorrow you will begin picking oakum at 6 o'clock in the morning.

Oliver   What's that, sir?

4th Gentleman of the Board
    Oakum is a fibre you get by picking old rope to pieces.

(Mr Bumble takes Oliver by the collar and leads him out. The four gentlemen exit. Oliver and the other workhouse boys take their place behind the long table which serves as a dining table in the workhouse. Each boy carries a bowl and spoon.)

N   Oliver joined a lot of other boys working in the workhouse. They had three meals of gruel every day. Gruel was a thin porridge which did not satisfy the boys hunger especially as they had to work hard every day.

(Workhouse man enters carrying a washing up bowl covered in brown sugar paper and a ladle. He stirs the bowl, mimes tasting it, pulls a face and spits it out. He then walks around giving each boy a ladleful. They eat it quickly. He exits.)

1st Boy   I'm hungry.

2nd Boy   I'm starving.

3rd Boy   If I don't get more to eat, I'm going to eat the boy in the bed next to me.

(The boys sitting next to him edge away looking scared.)

4th Boy	We should ask for more.
5th Boy	You ask for more.
4th Boy	I can't. I'm scared.
1st Boy	One of us ought to ask. (*To 4th Boy*) It's your idea, you ask.
2nd Boy	I know what to do. Let's all draw a straw out of a bale of hay. The one who pulls out the shortest straw has to ask.
N	That night when they went to their room to sleep, they each pulled out a straw and Oliver pulled out the shortest one. The next morning they all came down to breakfast.

(The workhouse man comes in and starts serving the gruel. The boys eat quickly and they all look at Oliver and nudge him. Oliver stands up and carries his bowl nervously up to the man.)

Man	What do you want?
Oliver	Please sir, I want some more.
Man	WHAT?
Oliver	Please sir, I want some more.
Man	MORE?

(He swings the ladle towards Oliver's head and knocks him backwards. Emphasize that he must not actually touch Oliver who immediately cries. He grabs Oliver and drags him off stage. One of the boys picks up the serving bowl and ladle and another boy picks up the bowls and spoons and takes them off-stage and they return to their seats.)

N	Oliver was then locked up and given to a local undertaker where he had to work and was treated just as cruelly.
N	In 'David Copperfield', Charles Dickens showed everyone how dreadful some schools were.

(Children as pupils sitting in desks in a line, chattering and making a noise and Mr Creakle comes in with a cane and glares. Boys become absolutely still and silent.)

Mr Creakle   Now boys, I advise you to come fresh to your lessons for I will come fresh with a punishment. There'll be no point in rubbing yourselves if I use this on you (*he swishes the cane and the boys stiffen*) for the marks I'll leave on you will not be easily rubbed away. Now get on with your work, all of you.

(Mr Creakle walks over to David Copperfield and glares at him.)

> I hear you're famous for biting, Copperfield. So am I. What do you think of that for a tooth? *(He pushes the cane in front of David's face)*
> Is it a sharp tooth? *(He swishes it in front of David)*
> Is it a long tooth? *(another swish)*
> Is it a double tooth? *(another swish)*
> Has it a deep prong? *(another swish)*
> Do you think it could cut deeply? *(He gives a cruel laugh and swishes it again as David starts to cry.)*
> Get on with your work, boys!

(The boys mime writing in absolute silence and Mr Creakle walks around and looks at their work.

Occasionally one looks up and he glares at him. Mr Creakle lifts David's slate and glares at it.)

Mr Creakle This is the worst writing I have ever seen. You will be punished for it and punished severely. Come with me.

(He takes David by the collar and leads him off out behind a curtain or out of sight.)

Bend over boy.

(He swishes the cane loudly so that everyone cringes and David howls after each one. David returns to the stage crying and rubbing his bottom. Mr Creakle exits.)

N Charles Dickens wrote another book called 'Nicholas Nickleby'. At a fearful school called Dotheboys Hall, he showed more of the gruesome treatment which boys got in a boarding school. Nicholas describes the school room as a bare and dirty room with two windows. About a tenth of the window space had glass in it and the rest was covered up with old pieces of paper. There were a couple of long broken-down tables, cut and notched and messed up with ink and damaged in every possible way.

(Mr Squeers walks up and down with his cane glaring at the boys while Mrs Squeers follows him with the basin and ladle giving the boys a dose. Their faces screw up on tasting it and they cough and choke and look sick.)

N Mr Squeers, the headmaster, was a horrid man. He walked around swishing his cane and poking children at every opportunity. His wife was even more unpleasant. She used to make a horrible tasting mixture of treacle and brimstone and used to force the unhappy boys to have a dose of it to purify their blood.

(Exit boys. Charles sits down to write.)

N Charles Dickens wrote other books to protest against the wrongs of his time. 'Bleak House' shows everyone how unfairly lawyers treated people who needed judgements in court.

N Charles Dickens wrote lots more books. He was delighted one day to see that the beautiful house Gad's Hill Place was for sale. He bought it and carried on his work there. In 1870 he had a stroke after working on his last book 'The Mystery of Edwin Drood'.

(Old Charles, sitting at his table, puts down his quill and mimes fainting with his head on the table.)

N He died the next day which was 14th June and was buried at Westminster Abbey.

N Let us pray.
Oh God, thank you for the life of Charles Dickens and his wonderful books which have given so much pleasure. Help us to use all our talents to improve life for ourselves and everyone else.

Chapter 9 Secular assemblies

Boudicca

d. c60AD

Although Boudicca died in despair and humiliation she is a revered character in our heritage. The history curriculum contains a unit on the Celts and the Roman invasions so an assembly on Boudicca is useful because it is an enjoyable way to reinforce your lessons.

> **Characters**
>
> Boudicca
> Prasutagus, her husband
> Their two daughters (non-speaking, but they can take narrators' parts)
> Suetonius Paulinus, the Roman military Governor
> Roman leader
> Roman messenger
> Celts
> Romans
> Lots of narrators who double up as Celts and Romans

(The children can stand in two groups, Romans and Celts, one at each side of the stage or the Romans off stage to begin. Narrators can be from either side.)

N   Our story begins in 500 BC.
     The Bronze Age people lived peacefully.
     In Britain there was a small population
     With plenty of space for the whole nation.

(Celts move to the front of the stage, walk on the spot, and look thoughtfully across the sea.)

N   In Europe lived the Celts, people of strong mettle
     Who wanted a new land where they could settle.
     They journeyed north of the coast of France
     Brave people they were happy to take a chance.

(Mime getting into boats and rowing and getting out and walking.)

N   In the distance they saw the cliffs of Dover.
     They jumped into boats and they sailed over
     The Channel and landed on Britain's coast.
     They were hard-working people and they made the most
     Of this new, exciting opportunity
     To build homes and thrive in their community.

N   They journeyed inland looking for high ground.
     They smoothed the land and dug ditches around

                          So they could build and live safe and sound.

(Lots of miming. Children spread out on the stage, some cutting down trees, sawing, some building, weaving the hazel rods round stakes, hunting in the forest and capturing boar and dragging them home, spinning and weaving, hammering iron, fishing.)

N   They went into the forest and cut down trees
                  And trimmed the branches off with ease.
                  And set the trunks to stand up tall
                  Around their fort to make a wall.

N   They marked perfect circles on the ground
                  And put in tree-trunks to make their round
                  Huts of wattle and daub attached
                  To strong and sturdy roofs of thatch.

N   They were clever hunters so off to the wood,
                  They trapped as many wild boar as they could
                  And brought them back to their fort with zeal
                  And used them to make a tasty meal.

N   They bred cattle and hens and horses and sheep.
                  They spun and wove their wool to keep
                  Themselves warm to work and sleep.
                  They were iron workers with plenty of skill
                  For making farmland tools to till
                  The land and grow barley and wheat
                  And fruit and vegetables to eat.

N   They were fishermen and boat builders too.
                  They thrived in Britain and their numbers grew.
                  For five hundred years the Celts kept arriving
                  In Britain and settling, building and thriving.

(Celts stop miming and exit.)

N   They lived in tribes with queens and kings.
                  Now this is where the action begins.

(Romans enter in neat rows and march on the spot with general in front. This is best done barefoot because the noise would drown out the speaker.)

                  In Europe, Roman rule was spreading.
                  Their well trained army legions were heading
                  Northward up through sunny France.
                  Right to the coast the army advanced.

N   They were fed up of the Celts' comings and goings
                  To help the Gauls opposed to the Romans.
                  And also they heard that Britain was rich
                  In iron and gold, so without a hitch
                  The Emperor ordered lots of legions
                  To invade and conquer as many regions
                  As they could, to add them to the empire.
                  And build up his treasure higher and higher.

(Romans mime entering their boats and rowing.)

N They packed up their boats and waited patiently
For the wind that would take them across the sea.
Some Celtic tribes were pleased at their arrival
The Romans could help some Celts' survival.

(The Romans get out of their boat and a few Celts shake hands with them.)

N They had plenty of wheat and wanted to trade.
They sold to the Romans who went off to raid
Some other tribes and leave them in peace.
But not every tribe was so pleased
To accept the Romans invading their land.
In East Anglia was a tribe who made a stand.

(Exit the Romans except the leader and one or two others. Enter Prasutagus, Boudicca and one or two Celts to meet them.)

N King Prasutagus was an elderly man
Who lived with Boudicca, his youthful wife.
She was tall and healthy and full of life
A woman who did not fear the strife.
Handsome and clever with deep red lips,
And long auburn hair flowing down to her hips.

N Prasutagus the Iceni tribe's wealthy king,
Realizing he couldn't have everything,
Talked to the Romans and made a sort of peace.
To make sure all fighting with them would cease.

Roman Leader
You can remain king as long as you live
On condition you and your tribesmen give
Taxes to Rome for the rest of your days
And on your death your heir pays
Half your wealth and land to the Emperor.
This agreement will ensure
The safety of the Iceni tribesmen.

Prasutagus
All right I agree. I'll make sure my men
Throughout all the Iceni regions
Do not attack the Roman legions.

(They shake hands and Romans exit. Enter the Celts.)

N So Prasutagus went home with his wife
Assured of peace for the rest of his life.
But after his death the Romans returned
And took half the money which the Celts had earned.
And as if that was not harsh enough
The Romans' sense of justice was rough.
The Romans took the Iceni's land.

(Roman army officer re-enters. Celts look furious.)

Roman Officer
                Prasutagus is dead. We are in command.

(He gives Celts a scornful look and exits.)

Boudicca   We must now act in swift defiance.
                I never had faith in that alliance.
                Let everyone rise up and follow me
                And show the Romans we'll have liberty.

(Enter Romans who grab Boudicca and her daughters and hold them with their arms spread-eagled and mime beating them with a whip.)

N   But the Romans never tolerated
                Being defied and berated,
                So Boudicca was humiliated.
                The Roman army was well equipped.
                Queen and daughters were speedily gripped
                Tied to stakes and publicly whipped.

Roman Army Officer *(Laughing)*
                That will teach that woman who's boss.
                A jolly good beating for those who cross
                The Roman army. We won't see her again.
                The job's well done. Come on men.

(Exit Romans. Boudicca and daughters hug and kiss each other and rub their aches and pains.)

N   But Boudicca was not an average girl.
                Eaten up with anger and in a whirl,
                Proud and filled with burning hate,
                Determined that she would create
                The greatest act of defiance yet.
                With swords and spears and blood and sweat,
                She ranted and charged every woman and man
                To drive the Romans out of their land.

N   They hadn't met a woman like her before
                And thought it perfectly safe to ignore
                Her angry threats and rants and wails
                Off they went to fight in North Wales.

Boudicca   *(Addressing the Celts)*
                Now that those devils are out of the way.
                We can beat them if we catch the day.
                Let's march off to Camulodunum
                We'll burn the place and kill the lot of them.

(Celts get into an untidy mob and follow Boudicca, walking on the spot, barefoot to mimimize sound.)

N   So at the head of a disorderly rabble.
                Eager and bloodthirsty for battle.
                They marched south with neighbouring tribes.
                Their bodies hot with vengeful vibes,
                Determined to burn, destroy and kill

	And fight to the last drop of blood until
	Those hateful, murdering Romans were gone
	And the Celts were free to live on and on.

(Celts spread out and mime attacking, stabbing a few Romans on the stage as victims but they must not touch a single Roman.)

N   Camulodunum was left undefended.
             The Celts did what they intended.
             They attacked the homes and temples and shops.
             With stabs and slashes and cracks and chops.
             The people ran and hid in the temple.

Boudicca Now is the time to make an example
             To show what happens to those who invade
             We too can pillage and wreck and raid!

N   And so our Boudicca had fire in her heart.

Boudicca We've not finished yet. It's only the start.
             Let's get on the road towards Londinium.
             We'll sack the place and have some fun.

(Disorderly rabble of Celts get into a bunch behind Boudicca to march, barefoot on the spot, to Londinium.)

N   And so the rowdy rabble came running
             With spears and swords, the sight was stunning.
             Yelling and cheering in delight and glee,
             Certain they were winning their liberty.

N   The Londinium road was straight and long.
             The Celts were certain they couldn't go wrong.
             When they arrived it was as they were hoping
             The gates weren't guarded and easy to open.

(Repeat mime of sacking the town.)

N   They forced their way in and stormed about
             Soon the citizens were driven out.
             They burned and battered and shattered and spoiled
             And left the city completely destroyed.

N   Another battle successfully won
             Satisfied with having the job well done,
             Boudicca called to her mischievous mob.

Boudicca Verulamium next. We've another job.

N   And next they headed for Watling Street
             Paving stones shaking beneath their feet.
             Until Verulamium was within their sight.
             The mob was relishing another fight.

N   And need I describe the sacking again.
             How this furious mob of women and men

Gave the terrified Romans a nasty taste
Of their own medicine as they laid waste
Their beautiful villas, statues and mosaics.
They wept and howled at their wounds and aches.

(Mime the sacking and exit Celts. Roman messenger mimes riding off to North Wales.)

N But where was the army, I'm sure you're wondering
Meanwhile a messenger's hooves were thundering
Up to North Wales with the dreadful story
Of Celtic raids all bloody and gory.

(Enter Suetonius and Romans to meet messenger who mimes speaking to Suetonius.)

N Suetonius the Roman governor raved.

Suetonius Our beautiful temples! Has nothing been saved?

(Calling to soldiers)
Pack up the kit, we are marching tonight.
We'll show the Celts how to pillage and fight.
Pack weapons and food. We'll need a load.
Get into line and get on the road.

(Romans line up in a neat orderly line to march on the spot. They must contrast with the disorderly Celts.)

N And leading his army all neatly in line.
Down Watling Street in double quick time.
Till the armies met, each raring to fight,
And completely destroy the other outright.

(Enter the Celts to meet them face to face. If possible Romans on stage and Celts in front of stage.)

Suetonius Listen up men. They cannot harm us.
They're only a rabble of women and farmers.
They're neither properly armed or trained.
She cannot control them. They are not restrained.
She has no battle plan. They'll run amok.
You are professional soldiers. They are in for a shock.
They are just a rabble milling around
And they haven't noticed, we've got the high ground.

Boudicca Good Celtic people listen to me.
We are fighting for our lost liberty!
We heavily outnumber them. We are bound to win.

(Celts rush on the spot shouting and yelling for about 5 seconds.)

N And before she could stop them they all rushed in
To battle, whooping and yelling like savages
Eager to start the battle ravages.
The Romans waited till they heard the command.
A spear flew out of each Roman hand.

(Romans mime throwing spears and some Celts mime being hit and falling. They then mime

fighting. Each Celt pairs up with a Roman and they mime fighting without actually touching each other. Gradually the Celts fall.)

N Unarmed the Celts fell one by one
As the viscious battle was begun.
When a Roman legion started getting tired
Suetonius called, and the soldiers retired
And immediately they were all replaced
And the Celts exhausted were scattered and spaced.

N Boudicca realized her army was finished
Eighty thousand men were now diminished.
All that was left was a sad battered crew.
There was only one thing that Boudicca could do.

(She takes the poison and hands it to her daughters and then drinks it herself.)

N She took poison from her belt and they drank.
Into a coma, Queen and daughters sank.
She died and the Romans took command
For a few more centuries they governed the land.

N These events were written down by two Roman historians called Tacitus and Dio Cassius. For many centuries the information was forgotten, but during the 16th century their writings were re-discovered and people became interested in Boudicca. Although she failed to drive the Romans out of Britain, she is remembered as a great warrior who made a heroic effort to defend the British against the invading Romans.

N Let us pray.
Oh God, let us never again have to go to war. Help everyone who governs us to see that it is better for all people to live in peace than to destroy each other in war. In the world today there are many wars. Please guide leaders to bring them all quickly to an end.

Chapter 9   Secular assemblies

Edith Cavell

1865 – 1915

Edith Cavell was a heroine of the First World War. Her story may be a suitable feature for a Remembrance Day assembly or just as a fine example of courage and devotion to one's country and fellow citizens.

> **Characters**
>
> Edith Cavell
> Rev Cavell, her father
> Mrs Cavell her mother
> Florence Cavell, her sister
> Lillian Cavell, her sister
> John Cavell, her brother
> Bishop Pelham
> Miss Eva Lückes
> Dr Depage
> Nurses
> Soldiers
> Interrogator
> Chaplain
> Narrators

(There is a group of chairs in a semicircle in the centre. A table and chair are at the side of the stage. Edith is seated writing a letter.)

N	Good morning and welcome to our assembly. Today 11th November, is Remembrance Day. Each year, on this day, we remember the thousands of people who died during the two World Wars of the twentieth century.
N	Today we are going to remember a nurse who worked with the wounded soldiers in Belgium and helped them to escape.
N	Edith Louisa Cavell was born in 1865, during the reign of Queen Victoria. Her father, Frederick Cavell, was the rector of a Swardeston Church in Norfolk. They were not rich but they lived in a fine Georgian vicarage. Frederick Cavell built another vicarage for the family, which was growing fast. The Cavells had three more children called Florence, Lillian and John.
N	Edith and her sisters did not go to school but had tutors in their home.
N	Edith was a happy lively girl. She loved to write letters.

Edith *(Reading)*
> Dear Cousin Eddie,
> I was delighted to receive your letter. I do hope you will come and stay with us sometime. Come during the week, not the week-end. Sunday is such a dull day. Father's sermons in church are so long and dull.
> Mother buys a joint of beef every Sunday and we are only allowed to eat half of it. The other half has to be given away to the poor.
> Father takes the fourth commandment very seriously. On Sundays we are not allowed to read anything except the Bible and we are not allowed to amuse ourselves with drawing or with even a game of cards. However, we do occasionally have a game in our bedrooms, when father is not in the house. During the week, Father is so different. He dresses up and plays with us. Last week he put on a bear costume and made us shriek with laughter.
> I'm pleased the winter is coming. Last year the moat at the old rectory froze over and we had such a lot of fun skating on it. I have been practising my painting a lot recently. I do love to set up my easel during the summer and paint the flowers on the common. Mother says my painting is improving.
> Do write soon, Eddie. We love to hear from you.
> Yours sincerely,
> Edith.

N Edith also loved to be busy supporting her parents in their church work.

(Enter Rev Cavell and Mrs Cavell)

Rev Cavell We need a Sunday School for the children of the parish but we haven't got a room for it. We need to build one but it will cost so much money and I have spent all my money building this vicarage.

Edith Perhaps the bishop could help. I'll write to him.

(She sits down at the table again and reads as she writes.)

Edith Dear Bishop Pelham
> I am writing about something very important to our church, Swardeston Parish in Norfolk. We have a lot of children in our church and would love to start a Sunday School for them but sadly we have no room to use for it. We need several hundred pounds to build one. We should be most grateful if the diocese could help. My mother, my sisters and I would love to teach in the Sunday School.
> I look forward to hearing from you.
> Yours sincerely,
> Edith Cavell

(She leaves the stage and the bishop enters. He sits down to write his reply. He reads it out as he writes.)

N The bishop was clearly impressed.

Bishop Pelham *(Writing)*
> Dear Miss Cavell,
> I am pleased to hear that you wish to be involved in such a worthwhile project. The diocese can help you but we should also like the parish to provide some of the money as well. If you can raise some money, the diocese will be pleased to assist you.
> Yours sincerely,
> John Pelham.

(Enter Edith, her mother and Florence.)

Edith	Look mother, a reply from the bishop. He is willing to give us some money for the Sunday School room as long as we raise some money ourselves. How shall we do it?

Florence	I know what we can do. We'll paint cards and sell them. *(They exit.)*

N	So the girls got to work painting and selling their work. They raised £300 for the Sunday School room and the bishop produced the rest so the Cavell family started their Sunday School. Edith was a Godmother to several children in the parish.

N	Today the east window of the Church is a memorial to Edith Cavell, for her hard work in the Sunday School.

N	Eventually, Edith and her sisters went off to boarding School. Edith loved dancing and playing tennis and eventually she became a pupil-teacher. Each day the pupils had a short lesson in conversational French and soon it was clear that Edith had a talent for it. She worked as a governess for several families and was loved by the children for her sense of fun and her kindness to them.

N	Around this time she was lucky to get a small legacy and she spent it on a continental holiday in Austria and Bavaria. During her stay there she visited a free hospital and was so impressed by it she gave it some of the money from her legacy.

N	In 1890, when she was 25, she decided to use her French and took a job with the François family in Brussels. During her holidays she returned home to Swardeston. Her family were always thrilled to see her back home.

(Enter Edith and her family who hug her and kiss her.)

Mrs Cavell	Welcome home Edith. We have missed you.

Florence	It's a lovely day. We must have a game of tennis.

Rev Cavell	There's plenty of canvas and paints in your room.

Florence	How is your French coming on?

Mrs Cavell	What are the family like?

Edith	They are very kind. I'm happy working there but it is lovely to be home.

(All exit, except Edith and Mrs Cavell)

N	In 1895, when she was thirty years old Edith returned home to Swardeston and helped to nurse her father who was ill.

Edith	You know, mother, I did like looking after father. I think I shall go and work in a hospital for a few months and, if I like it, I shall train as a nurse.

Mrs Cavell	I'm proud of you Edith. You'd make a wonderful nurse.

(Exit Mrs Cavell. Edith stands at the side of the stage. Enter Miss Lückes.)

N	Edith began her training at the London Hospital in 1896. Her trainer was Eva Lückes and she was a very strict taskmaster. She was not always impressed by Edith's efforts.

Miss Lückes *(To the audience)*
	Edith Louisa Cavell has plenty of capacity for her work, when she chooses to exert

herself. She does not put the effort in consistently and she is late, far too often.

(Exit Miss Lückes)

Edith *(Aside)*
Really I don't know what she is complaining about. We work from 7 a.m. until 9 p.m. with only half an hour off for lunch. And we are paid the wonderful sum of £10 per year.

N In spite of all of this, Edith's career as a nurse moved swiftly. She did private nursing for a year and then worked at the St Pancras Hospital with people who were homeless.

N She went to the Shoreditch Infirmary where she became the Assistant Matron when she was thirty-seven. She started the practice of visiting patients after they left hospital.

N In 1906 when she was almost forty, Edith went to work in Manchester and Salford in the Queen's District Nursing Homes and she soon became the Matron.

N In 1907, she went to work in Brussels again to nurse a child who was a patient of Dr Antoine Depage. He was impressed with her.

(Enter Dr Depage)

Dr Depage We would like to start training nurses to work similarly to the way of Florence Nightingale. We think you would be the ideal person to be in charge of the work. We have four adjoining houses for the training school. We would be honoured if you would take the job.

Edith I would be delighted. I shall start as soon as it is possible.

N Edith loved the work and her holidays at home with her family in England. On one holiday in 1914...

(Edith arriving home, hugs and kisses her family and then they sit down on the chairs centre stage to hear about Edith's work.)

Mrs Cavell Tell us all about your work, Edith.

Edith I'm really enjoying it, Mother. I have four houses to work in. I give lectures to nurses and doctors a few times a week. I train nurses for hospitals and schools and kindergartens.

Florence *(Laughing)*
And do your nurses please you more than you used to please Miss Lückes?

Edith Oh Florence, Miss Lückes wouldn't believe it if she saw me. I keep a watch on my breakfast table and if any nurse is more than two minutes late, I make her lose two hours of her spare time.

Lillian I'm glad I don't work for you, Edith.

John Is it easy to find women who want to become nurses?

Edith Sometimes it's hard. It's a bit like England has been in the past. Some women, who come from better off homes, still think it is a disgrace to have to earn their own living.

Lillian How do you persuade them?

Edith Well, recently the Queen of Belgium broke her arm and came to the school for treatment and so now people think more highly of us.

John We have a new wireless, Edith. Let's turn it on and hear the news.

(He gets up and mimes turning on the radio.)

Radio voice This is the six o'clock news. Today the German army invaded Belgium.

Edith Oh no that's awful.

John *(Turning off the radio)* Oh well, Edith, you can't go back now.

Edith Of course I can.

Florence Surely not. It will be dangerous.

Mrs Cavell Oh please stay at home, Edith. We can't bear to think of you being killed.

Edith Now that this has happened it is more important than ever that I return.

(They exit, each taking their chair with them. Enter lots of nurses.)

N So Edith returned to Belgium. Her clinic became a Red Cross Hospital and immediately they had masses of patients.

Edith *(Addressing a lot of nurses)*
And remember, nurses, we are Red Cross nurses. Our duty is to treat all wounded people of every nationality. It makes no difference whether a soldier is British or Belgian or German, we must treat them all the same.

N However, this did not last long. Within months the Germans had taken over Belgium and most of the British nurses were sent home. Only Edith and her deputy stayed. One day two British soldiers arrived at her training school.

(Exit the nurses, except Edith and one other. Enter two wounded soldiers.)

Soldier We have escaped but we have to get out of Belgium and into Holland before the Germans find us.

Edith Thank goodness you came here. We can hide you for a while but we must find a way to get you out.

(All exit)

N In the months that followed, other soldiers came to Edith Cavell's school. Philippe Bacqu an architect, and the Prince and Princess of Croy helped her to set up a secret organization to help soldiers to escape from Belgium.

N This was a brave thing to do. Edith was protected under the law because she was a Red Cross nurse, but this meant she was not allowed to help any one nationality more than another, and certainly not allowed to help British soldiers to escape from the Germans. Edith was breaking the rules but she decided to help her fellow country men.

(Enter Edith and soldier)

Soldier Nurse Cavell, I am wounded. Can you help me?

Edith Of course, but come through to the back. The Germans often come round searching.

Soldier *(Looking around).* Thank you for your help. That's a beautiful picture of Norwich Cathedral on your wall.

Edith Oh do you know it? I am from Norfolk.

Soldier	So am I.
Edith	I'm delighted to meet someone from my county. May I give you a letter to deliver to my mother when you return to England?
Soldier	Yes, of course. I'd be pleased to do that for you. Do your other nurses know that you help soldiers to escape?
Edith	No. I'm breaking the rules. If I get caught it is safer for the other nurses not to know.
Soldier	You are a very brave woman.
Edith	I am a nurse who is doing my duty. That's all.
N	Eventually Edith was found out. The German authorities were told of her helping soldiers to escape and they searched her training school. As they arrived a soldier managed to slip out the back.
N	Edith and the other members of the escape party were arrested and questioned.
Interrogator	You are accused of helping British soldiers to escape. We have arrested your friends who helped you in this crime. They have confessed that you helped them to assist soldiers to escape. Do you admit that you are guilty of this crime.
Edith	Yes. *(Exit interrogator. Enter Chaplain. He takes her hand.)*
N	Edith was shot the next day. The evening before she was shot by the firing squad, the English chaplain came to visit her. She was very calm and accepted her punishment. She said...
Edith	I am thankful to have had these ten weeks of quiet to get ready. Now I have had them and have been kindly treated here. I expected my sentence and I believe it was just. Standing as I do in view of God and Eternity, I realize that patriotism is not enough. I must have no hatred or bitterness towards anyone.
N	The next day, Edith was shot. There was an outcry against such a harsh punishment. She was buried and a plain cross put over her grave. After the war, her remains were dug up and returned to England. There was a burial service for her at Westminster Abbey and Queen Alexandra attended it. Next her body was taken to Norwich Cathedral where it is buried today.
N	Edith Cavell is not forgotten in her home parish of Swardeston. The church always has a beautiful display of flowers remembering how much Edith loved them and every two years the church holds a Flower Festival commemorating her life.
N	Let us pray. Oh God, we thank you for the life of Edith Cavell and all the brave people who have devoted their lives to helping others during both World Wars. We ask that it will never be necessary for our country to go to war again and ask you to bring peace to all the war-torn areas of the world.

Bibliography

Barron, S (2002) *Great Religious Leaders – Moses and Judaism*. Hodder Wayland. Lewes
Chambers, C. (1995) *Beliefs and Cultures – Sikh*. Watts Books. London
Dhanjal, B. (1996) *What do we know about Sikhism?* Hodder Wayland. London
Ganeri, A. (1996) *Beliefs and Cultures – Buddhist*. Franklin Watts. London
Middleton, H. (2001) *Profiles – Mother Teresa*. Heineman
Penney, S. (1996) *Discovering Religions – Sikhism*. Heineman. Oxford
Penny, S. (1987) *Discovering Religions – Judaism*. Heineman. Oxford
Rose, D. and G. (1997) *A World of Festivals – Passover*. Evans Brothers Ltd. London
Tames, R. (1989) *Lifetimes – Mother Teresa*. Franklin Watts
Teece, G. (2003) *Religion in Focus – Buddhism*. Franklin Watts. London
Children's Britannica (1985) *Encyclopaedia International Ltd*. London
The Holy Bible